CW00802543

Module E(S) – Contents

The suggested answers presented in this booklet are longer and generally more detailed than those expected from a candidate taking the examinations. These answers are intended to provide candidates should try to provide. The suggested answer may not contain all the points that could correctly be made and candidates should note that credit will be awarded for valid answers which may not be fully covered in this booklet.

Typeset by Pindar plc, Scarborough, North Yorkshire.
Printed by Bell & Bain Ltd., Glasgow

Module E – Professional Stage

Information for Control and Decision Making

June 1996

Question Paper:	
Time allowed	**3 hours**
This paper is divided into two sections	
Section A	TWO questions ONLY to be answered
Section B	TWO questions ONLY to be answered
Present value table and Annuity table are on pages 12 and 13	

Section A – TWO questions ONLY to be attempted

1   Leano plc is investigating the financial viability of a new product X. Product X is a short life product for which a market has been identified at an agreed design specification. It is not yet clear whether the market life of the product will be six months or 12 months.

The following estimated information is available in respect of product X:

(i)   Sales should be 10,000 units per month in batches of 100 units on a just-in-time production basis. An average selling price of £1,200 per batch of 100 units is expected for a six month life cycle and £1,050 per batch of 100 units for a 12 month life cycle.

(ii) An 80% learning curve will apply in months 1 to 7 (inclusive), after which a steady state production time requirement will apply, with labour time per batch stabilising at that of the final batch in month 7. Reductions in the labour requirement will be achieved through natural labour turnover. The labour requirement for the first batch in month 1 will be 500 hours at £5 per hour.

(iii) Variable overhead is estimated at £2 per labour hour.

(iv) Direct material input will be £500 per batch of product X for the first 200 batches. The next 200 batches are expected to cost 90% of the initial batch cost. All batches thereafter will cost 90% of the batch cost for each of the second 200 batches.

(v)   Product X will incur directly attributable fixed costs of £15,000 per month.

(vi) The initial investment for the new product will be £75,000 with no residual value irrespective of the life of the product.

A target cash inflow required over the life of the product must be sufficient to provide for:

(a)   the initial investment plus 33 1/3% thereof for a six month life cycle, or

(b)   the initial investment plus 50% thereof for a 12 month life cycle.

Note: learning curve formula:
$$y = ax^b$$
where y = average cost per batch

a = cost of initial batch

x = total number of batches

b = learning factor (= −0·3219 for 80% learning rate)

Required:

(a) Prepare detailed calculations to show whether product X will provide the target cash inflow over six months and/or 12 months.

(17 marks)

(b) Calculate the initial batch labour hours at which the cash inflow achieved will be exactly equal to the target figure where a six month life cycle applies. It has been determined that the maximum labour and variable overhead cost at which the target return will be achieved is £259,000. All other variables remain as in part (a).

(6 marks)

(c) Prepare a report to management which:

(i) explains why the product X proposal is an example of a target costing/pricing situation; (3 marks)

(ii) suggests specific actions which may be considered to improve the return on investment where a six month product cycle is forecast; (6 marks)

(iii) comments on possible factors which could reduce the rate of return and which must, therefore, be avoided. (3 marks)

(35 marks)

2 Easterpark Division is considering an investment opportunity to which the following information relates:

(i) Initial investment of £6,000,000 with a project life of five years and nil residual value. Straight-line depreciation is used.

(ii) The project will provide 4,800 hours of process time per annum, the chargeable proportion of which will have a likely contribution of £500 per chargeable hour.

(iii) The required return (cost of capital) is estimated at 10%. *Ignore taxation.*

(iv) Tables 1 and 2 are part of the output of a spreadsheet model using the variable input data provided in the question.

Required:

(a) Discuss the acceptability of the proposal using the data in the question and Tables 1 and 2. You should take into account the range of performance measures available and the likelihood that management will tend to take a short-term view because of a group policy of rapid management turnover at each division as part of a career development programme. (10 marks)

(b) (i) Calculate and present the year 1 and year 2 figures from Table 1 where annuity depreciation is used, based on a cost of capital of 10%. (8 marks)

(ii) Comment on the acceptability of the revised figures produced in (b)(i) and their impact on management decision-making in relation to the investment proposal. (4 marks)

(c) Explain (with relevant calculations) the approximate relationship between the residual incomes over the five-year period and net present value of the investment stated in Table 1. (3 marks)

4

(d) (i) The proportion of process time able to be converted into chargeable output will be linked to a decision on annual maintenance expenditure. The incremental and total annual maintenance cost and the incremental percentage of process time which will be available as chargeable where such maintenance is implemented is as follows:

Maintenance level	Chargeable proportion of process time %	Incremental cost £	Total cost £
1	77·5	260,000	260,000
2	8·0	100,000	360,000
3	2·5	80,000	440,000

All three levels of maintenance cost are currently implemented in the evaluation of the proposal in Tables 1 and 2.

Determine whether implementing maintenance at level 1 only OR at level 1 plus level 2 only, will improve the profitability of the proposal per annum when the contribution is £500 per chargeable hour. (4 marks)

(ii) Explain the process of introducing a zero-based budgeting exercise at Easterpark Division and how such an exercise could affect the implementation of the decision in (d)(i) above. (6 marks)

(35 marks)

Table 1

Financial evaluation of the investment where straight-line depreciation is in use

	year 1 £	year 2 £	year 3 £	year 4 £	year 5 £
Investment (WDV at beginning of year)	6,000,000	4,800,000	3,600,000	2,400,000	1,200,000
Contribution	2,112,000	2,112,000	2,112,000	2,112,000	2,112,000
Less maintenance cost	440,000	440,000	440,000	440,000	440,000
Net margin	1,672,000	1,672,000	1,672,000	1,672,000	1,672,000
Less depreciation	1,200,000	1,200,000	1,200,000	1,200,000	1,200,000
Net profit	472,000	472,000	472,000	472,000	472,000
Less imputed interest at 10%	600,000	480,000	360,000	240,000	120,000
Residual income	−128,000	−8,000	112,000	232,000	352,000
Return on investment (%)	7·9%	9·8%	13·1%	19·7%	39·3%

NPV of investment (£) at 10% | 338,552 |

Table 2

Contribution per hour £	Net profit £	Residual income £	ROI	NPV £
	Year 1 values for various performance measures where straight-line depreciation is in use			Over 5 year life
450	260,800	–339,200	4·3%	–462,107
460	303,040	–296,960	5·1%	–301,975
470	345,280	–254,720	5·8%	–141,844
480	387,520	–212,480	6·5%	18,288
490	429,760	–170,240	7·2%	178,420
500	472,000	–128,000	7·9%	338,552
510	514,240	–85,760	8·6%	498,684
520	556,480	–43,520	9·3%	658,816
530	598,720	–1,280	10·0%	818,948
540	640,960	40,960	10·7%	979,079
550	683,200	83,200	11·4%	1,139,211

3 EVCO plc produces and sells a single product by passing a single raw material through three consecutive production processes – making, converting and finishing. A system of standard process costing is in operation for which the following information is available for the period ended 30 April 1996:

(i) Stocks are held at constant levels at the beginning and end of the period as follows: raw material (4,000 kg at £0·75 per kg); WIP – converting (500 units); WIP – finishing (500 units); finished goods (500 units).

(ii) Process accounts are debited with the actual costs incurred for the period.

(iii) All losses and transfers between processes or into finished goods are valued at standard cost at their stage of completion. Such unit standard costs may be determined from the information in Table A.

(iv) WIP in converting and finishing is held at the beginning of each process.

(v) The units transferred into finished goods will eventually comprise free replacements to customers, finished goods stock losses and the balance as net sales to customers.

Table B shows the summary profit and loss account for the period ended 30 April 1996 showing budget and actual analysis of gross profit/(loss).

Information relevant to the profit and loss account is as follows:

(i) Free replacements to customers and finished goods stock losses are valued at standard cost per unit.

(ii) The price reduction penalty is allowable on goods delivered late to customers at 5% of the normal selling price of £30 per unit.

EVCO plc presently relies on the variances (£) reported in its standard process system as its main source of control information.

Required:

(a) Prepare accounts for the period ended 30 April 1996 using 'back-flush accounting' instead of the present system. The accounts required are (i) raw materials and in-process account (ii) finished goods stock account. (10 marks)

(b) Discuss the merits of the use of the backflush accounting procedure in EVCO plc as in (a) above. (5 marks)

(c) Prepare a report for the period ended 30 April 1996 to the management team of EVCO plc which:

(i) details the factors which have contributed to the poor performance of EVCO plc. (6 marks)

(ii) **expresses budget and actual levels (units and percentage) for each of the following as examples of non-financial indicators of performance:**

- **free replacements to customers (compared to units delivered)**
- **late deliveries to customers (against net sales units)**
- **finished goods stock losses (compared to stock level)**

(6 marks)

(Show all relevant workings)

(iii) **suggests features of a total quality programme which should help EVCO plc to overcome the present poor level of performance.** (8 marks)

(35 marks)

Table A

EVCO plc: Standard process accounts for the period ended 30 April 1996

	Making process		Converting process		Finishing process	
	Product units	£	Product units	£	Product units	£
DR						
WIP b/f			500	7,909	500	10,054
Transfers from previous process			6,800	107,563	6,025	121,156
Raw material cost	8,000	96,000				
Conversion costs		18,800		30,100		14,390
	8,000	114,800	7,300	145,572	6,525	145,600
CR.						
Normal losses	800		504		298	
Transfers to next process	6,800	107,563	6,025	121,156	5,365	124,655
WIP damage (written off)			75	1,186	60	1,207
Abnormal process losses	400	6,327	196	3,934	302	6,822
Residual variance		910		11,387		2,862
WIP, c/f			500	7,909	500	10,054
	8,000	114,800	7,300	145,572	6,525	145,600

Table B

EVCO plc: Summary profit and loss account for the period ended 30 April 1996

	Actual £	Actual £	Budget £	Budget £
Sales revenue		145,050		150,000
Less standard cost of sales		112,341		116,175
Standard contribution		32,709		33,825
Less: WIP damage losses	2,393		1,437	
Finished goods losses	697		232	
Abnormal losses	17,083			
Residual process variances	15,159			
Free replacements to customers	11,617		4,832	
Price reduction penalty	1,160		750	
Raw material stock damage losses	240		120	
		48,349		7,371
Gross profit/(loss)		(15,640)		26,454

Section B – TWO questions ONLY to be attempted

4 A bank has a section of its business which has two functions:

1. answering credit control queries from customers both by telephone and in writing;

2. investment business queries involving responding by telephone and in writing about surrender values, assignment of policies and maturity value quotations.

The staff are arranged in four workgroups, one for each of four geographical areas. Each workgroup consists of 30 employees plus supervisor. Each employee is expected to answer telephone enquiries and a proportion of written enquiries for both credit control and investment business.

Flexi-time working is allowed and considerable overtime is paid in addition to a basic salary payment. There is a high backlog of written enquiries and customers have been complaining about poor telephone response times and quality of response. High staff turnover exists and staff morale is low.

As management accountant you are part of a team required to investigate and report on performance measurement and effectiveness of operations.

Required:

(a) Explain, giving examples of their incidence in the provision of the above services, any THREE of the following.

(i) intangibility

(ii) heterogeneity

(iii) simultaneity

(iv) perishability (8 marks)

(b) Suggest a possible reorganisation of the workforce into a team or 'cell' structure and discuss the advantages which such a system may have over the existing situation. (7 marks)

(15 marks)

5 (a) 'It may be argued that in a total quality environment, variance analysis from a standard costing system is redundant.'

Discuss the validity of this statement. (8 marks)

(b) Using labour cost as the focus, discuss the differences in the measurement of labour efficiency/effectiveness where (i) total quality management techniques and (ii) standard cost variance analysis are implemented. (7 marks)

(15 marks)

6   Istana Division is part of the Marmaris Group. Istana Division produces a single product for which it has an external market which utilises 80% of its production capacity.

Taman Division, which is also part of the Marmaris Group, requires units of the product available from Istana Division as input to a product which will be sold outside of the group. Taman Division's requirements are equal to 40% of Istana Division's production capacity.

Taman Division has a potential source of supply from outside the Marmaris Group. This outside supplier can supply 75% of Taman Division's requirement. The outside source may wish to quote a higher price if Taman Division only intends to take up part of its product availability.

Required:

Discuss aspects of transfer pricing principles and information availability which will affect the likely achievement of group profit maximisation from the sourcing decisions made by Taman Division in the above situation.

(15 marks)

[P.T.O.

Present value table

Present value of 1 i.e. $(1 + r)^{-n}$

where r = discount rate
n = number of periods until payment

Discount rates (r)

Periods (n)	1%	2%	3%	4%	5%	6%	7%	8%	9%	10%	
1	0·990	0·980	0·971	0·962	0·952	0·943	0·935	0·926	0·917	0·909	1
2	0·980	0·961	0·943	0·925	0·907	0·890	0·873	0·857	0·842	0·826	2
3	0·971	0·942	0·915	0·889	0·864	0·840	0·816	0·794	0·772	0·751	3
4	0·961	0·924	0·888	0·855	0·823	0·792	0·763	0·735	0·708	0·683	4
5	0·951	0·906	0·863	0·822	0·784	0·747	0·713	0·681	0·650	0·621	5
6	0·942	0·888	0·837	0·790	0·746	0·705	0·666	0·630	0·596	0·564	6
7	0·933	0·871	0·813	0·760	0·711	0·665	0·623	0·583	0·547	0·513	7
8	0·923	0·853	0·789	0·731	0·677	0·627	0·582	0·540	0·502	0·467	8
9	0·941	0·837	0·766	0·703	0·645	0·592	0·544	0·500	0·460	0·424	9
10	0·905	0·820	0·744	0·676	0·614	0·558	0·508	0·463	0·422	0·386	10
11	0·896	0·804	0·722	0·650	0·585	0·527	0·475	0·429	0·388	0·350	11
12	0·887	0·788	0·701	0·625	0·557	0·497	0·444	0·397	0·356	0·319	12
13	0·879	0·773	0·681	0·601	0·530	0·469	0·415	0·368	0·326	0·290	13
14	0·870	0·758	0·661	0·577	0·505	0·442	0·388	0·340	0·299	0·263	14
15	0·861	0·743	0·642	0·555	0·481	0·417	0·362	0·315	0·275	0·239	15

	11%	12%	13%	14%	15%	16%	17%	18%	19%	20%	
1	0·901	0·893	0·885	0·877	0·870	0·862	0·855	0·847	0·840	0·833	1
2	0·812	0·797	0·783	0·769	0·756	0·743	0·731	0·718	0·706	0·694	2
3	0·731	0·712	0·693	0·675	0·658	0·641	0·624	0·609	0·593	0·579	3
4	0·659	0·636	0·613	0·592	0·572	0·552	0·534	0·516	0·499	0·482	4
5	0·593	0·567	0·543	0·519	0·497	0·476	0·456	0·437	0·419	0·402	5
6	0·535	0·507	0·480	0·456	0·432	0·410	0·390	0·370	0·352	0·335	6
7	0·482	0·452	0·425	0·400	0·376	0·354	0·333	0·314	0·296	0·279	7
8	0·434	0·404	0·376	0·351	0·327	0·305	0·285	0·266	0·249	0·233	8
9	0·391	0·361	0·333	0·308	0·284	0·263	0·243	0·225	0·209	0·194	9
10	0·352	0·322	0·295	0·270	0·247	0·227	0·208	0·191	0·176	0·162	10
11	0·317	0·287	0·261	0·237	0·215	0·195	0·178	0·162	0·148	0·135	11
12	0·286	0·257	0·231	0·208	0·187	0·168	0·152	0·137	0·124	0·112	12
13	0·258	0·229	0·204	0·182	0·163	0·145	0·130	0·116	0·104	0·093	13
14	0·232	0·205	0·181	0·160	0·141	0·125	0·111	0·099	0·088	0·078	14
15	0·209	0·183	0·160	0·140	0·123	0·108	0·095	0·084	0·074	0·065	15

Annuity Table

Present value of an annuity of 1 i.e. $\dfrac{1 - (1 + r)^{-n}}{r}$

where r = interest rate
$\quad\quad\, n$ = number of periods

Interest rates (r)

Periods

(n)	1%	2%	3%	4%	5%	6%	7%	8%	9%	10%	
1	0·990	0·980	0·971	0·962	0·952	0·943	0·935	0·926	0·917	0·909	1
2	1·970	1·942	1·913	1·886	1·859	1·833	1·808	1·783	1·759	1·736	2
3	2·941	2·884	2·829	2·775	2·723	2·673	2·624	2·577	2·531	2·487	3
4	3·902	3·808	3·717	3·630	3·546	3·465	3·387	3·312	3·240	3·170	4
5	4·853	4·713	4·580	4·452	4·329	4·212	4·100	3·993	3·890	3·791	5
6	5·795	5·601	5·417	5·242	5·076	4·917	4·767	4·623	4·486	4·355	6
7	6·728	6·472	6·230	6·002	5·786	5·582	5·389	5·206	5·033	4·868	7
8	7·652	7·325	7·020	6·733	6·463	6·210	5·971	5·747	5·535	5·335	8
9	8·566	8·162	7·786	7·435	7·108	6·802	6·515	6·247	5·995	5·759	9
10	9·471	8·983	8·530	8·111	7·722	7·360	7·024	6·710	6·418	6·145	10
11	10·37	9·787	9·253	8·760	8·306	7·887	7·499	7·139	6·805	6·495	11
12	11·26	10·58	9·954	9·385	8·863	8·384	7·943	7·536	7·161	6·814	12
13	12·13	11·35	10·63	9·986	9·394	8·853	8·358	7·904	7·487	7·103	13
14	13·00	12·11	11·30	10·56	9·899	9·295	8·745	8·244	7·786	7·367	14
15	13·87	12·85	11·94	11·12	10·38	9·712	9·108	8·559	8·061	7·606	15

	11%	12%	13%	14%	15%	16%	17%	18%	19%	20%	
1	0·901	0·893	0·885	0·877	0·870	0·862	0·855	0·847	0·840	0·833	1
2	1·713	1·690	1·668	1·647	1·626	1·605	1·585	1·566	1·547	1·528	2
3	2·444	2·402	2·361	2·322	2·283	2·246	2·210	2·174	2·140	2·106	3
4	3·102	3·037	2·974	2·914	2·855	2·798	2·743	2·690	2·639	2·589	4
5	3·696	3·605	3·517	3·433	3·352	3·274	3·199	3·127	3·058	2·991	5
6	4·231	4·111	3·998	3·889	3·784	3·685	3·589	3·498	3·410	3·326	6
7	4·712	4·564	4·423	4·288	4·160	4·039	3·922	3·812	3·706	3·605	7
8	5·146	4·968	4·799	4·639	4·487	4·344	4·207	4·078	3·954	3·837	8
9	5·537	5·328	5·132	4·946	4·772	4·607	4·451	4·303	4·163	4·031	9
10	5·889	5·650	5·426	5·216	5·019	4·833	4·659	4·494	4·339	4·192	10
11	6·207	5·938	5·687	5·453	5·234	5·029	4·836	4·656	4·486	4·327	11
12	6·492	6·194	5·918	5·660	5·421	5·197	4·988	4·793	4·611	4·439	12
13	6·750	6·424	6·122	5·842	5·583	5·342	5·118	4·910	4·715	4·533	13
14	6·982	6·628	6·302	6·002	5·724	5·468	5·229	5·008	4·802	4·611	14
15	7·191	6·811	6·462	6·142	5·847	5·575	5·324	5·092	4·876	4·675	15

End of Question Paper

Answers

1   (a)

	6 months	12 months
Sales units	60,000	120,000
	£	£
Sales revenue (1)	720,000	1,260,000
Costs:		
Direct material (2)	271,000	514,000
Direct labour (3)	191,340	315,423
Variable overhead (4)	76,536	126,169
DAFC	90,000	180,000
	628,876	1,135,592
Net cash inflow	91,124	124,408

Required cash inflow for target return:

£75,000 + 33·33%	£100,000
£75,000 + 50%	£112,500

The target return will be achieved over a 12 month life cycle.

Working notes:

1. Sales for six months and 12 months are at £1,200 and £1,050 per batch of 100 units respectively.

2. Direct material:

batches	£
200 × £500	100,000
200 × £450	90,000
200 × £405	81,000
for six months	271,000
600 × £405	243,000
for 12 months	514,000

3. Direct labour:

For first six months:
$$y = ax^b$$
$$= 2,500 \times 600^{-0.3219}$$
$$= £318.90$$

Hence total cost = £318·90 × 600 batches = £191,340

For seven months:
$$y = ax^b$$
$$= 2,500 \times 700^{-0.3219}$$
$$= £303.461$$

Hence total cost = £303·461 × 700 batches = £212,423

All batches after the first 700 will have the labour cost of the 700th batch.

For 699 batches:
$$y = ax^b$$
$$= 2,500 \times 699^{-0.3219}$$
$$= £303.601$$

Hence total cost = £303·601 × 699 batches = £212,217

Cost of 700th batch = £212,423 – £212,217 = £206

Total cost for 12 months = £212,423 + (£206 × 500) = £315,423

4. Variable overhead is £2 per hour i.e. 40% of direct labour.

(b) Variable overhead is dependent on labour cost.

To achieve the target return of £100,000 in the six months, labour and overhead must be reduced by the current shortfall of £8,876.

Maximum labour and overhead = £259,000

let y = average labour cost per batch of product

We require 1·4 × 600 × y = £259,000

Solving y = £308·333

Now learning curve is $y = ax^b$

Substituting $\qquad 308.33 = a \times 600^{-0.3219}$

$\qquad\qquad a \qquad = £2,417$ (approx.)

Hence initial batch labour hours = £2,417/£5 = 483·4 hours (approx.)

(c)

Leano plc

Report on new product proposal

(i) The proposal for the new short life product X is an example of target costing/pricing in that the cycle is such that:

- the market has been identified in terms of quantity and price

- the required rate of return over the life of the product has been set

- the need to ensure that costs can be restructured in order to provide the required return over six months has been evaluated.

(ii) A number of specific actions may be considered in order to improve the return on investment:

- reduce the initial labour cost per batch by examination of the production process with a view to the elimination of unnecessary operations.

- improve the learning curve rate, possibly by additional training or change in the method of production

- reduce the material losses in the early batches prior to the steady state being reached

- examine the variable overhead element which is being absorbed per labour hour. Is labour hours the sole and/or most relevant cost driver?

- investigate whether the £15,000 per month of DAFC contains any non-value added overheads which may be eliminated

- investigate whether any of the DAFC may be sourced more cheaply.

(iii) All of the above must be considered taking into account the need to provide a product of the agreed design specification and performance, otherwise free replacements of faulty units to the customer and/or warranty claims may reduce the return from the product.

A Person

Management Accountant

June 1996

2   (a) A range of financial performance measures are available for the Easterpark investment opportunity. Return on investment (ROI) and residual income (RI) may be viewed in the short or longer term. Where a short-term view is taken, as may be by Easterpark management, ROI (7·9%) is less than the cost of capital (10%) in year 1 and again in year 2 (9·8%). Similarly, RI in year 1 is negative (–£128,000) and again in year 2 (–£8,000). Both of these measures will lead to the rejection of the proposal on financial grounds where a short-term view is taken in the decision process. In the longer term both ROI and RI are acceptable.

Table 1 shows that on a discounted cash flow basis over the life of the proposal a positive NPV of £338,552 is reported which would make it viable where the cost of capital is 10%.

Table 2 shows the impact of change in the contribution per hour on the interpretation of each performance measure for year 1 (or for NPV). The proposal is still financially viable where NPV is used even if contribution falls to £480 per hour.

In the short term residual income would only indicate acceptance of the proposal where contribution per hour was £540 or more. Return on investment (based on year 1) would indicate acceptance where contribution per hour was £530 or more.

(b) (i)

Using annuity depreciation:

	Year 1	Year 2
	£	£
Investment (WDV at beginning of year)	6,000,000	5,017,304
Contribution	2,112,000	2,112,000
Less maintenance cost	440,000	440,000
Net margin	1,672,000	1,672,000
Less depreciation	982,696	1,080,966
Net profit	689,304	591,034
Less imputed interest	600,000	501,730
Residual income	89,304	89,304
Return on investment%	11·5%	11·8%

Working notes:

Required annual equivalent cash inflow = £6,000,000/3·791 = £1,582,696

For year 1: imputed interest = 10% × £6,000,000 = £600,000

depreciation = £1,582,696 − £600,000 = £982,696

For year 2: investment WDV = £6,000,000 − £982,696 = £5,017,304

imputed interest = 10% × £5,017,304 = £501,730

depreciation = £1,582,696 − £501,730 = £1,080,966

(ii) The use of annuity depreciation for the calculation of ROI and RI will make the proposal acceptable even in the short term where these measures are used. RI is equalised at £89,304 in each year. ROI is now in excess of the required return of 10% even in year 1, due to the adjusted depreciation charge.

A problem with the use of annuity depreciation in the calculations is that it is unlikely to be used in practice as part of the financial reporting system.

(c) The discounted value of the residual income = NPV.

year	RI £	DCF factor	Discounted cash flow £
1	−128,000	0·909	−116,352
2	−8,000	0·826	−6,608
3	112,000	0·751	84,112
4	232,000	0·683	158,456
5	352,000	0·621	218,592
	NPV		338,200

This differs slightly from the NPV shown in Table 1 (£338,552) because of a slight difference in the Annuity Table and Present Value Table values used when discounting the cash flows.

This confirms that the residual income value is the excess cash inflow available over that required to provide a return equivalent to the cost of capital.

(d) **(i)** Incremental hours at level 2 = 4,800 × 8% = 384 hours

Incremental hours at level 3 = 4,800 × 2·5% = 120 hours

Now incremental gain/(loss) = incremental contribution − incremental cost

At level 2 = (384 × £500) − £100,000 = £92,000

At level 3 = (120 × £500) − £80,000 = (£20,000)

This means that incorporating maintenance at level 1 only will result in a net fall in profit of £72,000 from the present level. Incorporating maintenance at level 1 + level 2 will result in a net increase in profit of £20,000 over the present level.

(ii) The principles and steps in introducing zero-base budgeting may be summarised as:

- it rejects the idea that the current model/strategy is the best
- it requires incremental packages of activity for each function – such as maintenance – to be evaluated
- it is up to the function manager to put the best possible case for each incremental package
- each function will then compete with others for a share of available budget funds.

The final decision may rely on the strength of argument put by the maintenance manager.

For Easterpark Division, maintenance is possibly one of a number of services competing for funds. The maintenance manager may lose out on level 2 even though it will add to company profitability. This would make the proposal less attractive in financial terms.

Alternatively the manager may be able to argue the case for the inclusion of level 3 even though it would result in an incremental loss of £20,000, if he can convince management of intangible benefits such as long-term ability to sustain market share.

3   (a)   *Materials and in-process account*

	£		£
Material and in-process stock b/f	20,963	To finished goods (at standard)	124,655
Variable costs:		Residual variances	34,635
Material cost	96,000	Material and in-process stock c/f	20,963
Conversion cost	63,290		
	180,253		180,253

Finished goods account

	£		£
Finished goods stock b/f	11,618	To cost of sales (P/L)	112,341
Ex-materials and in-process account	124,655	Free replacements (P/L)	11,617
		Stock losses written off (P/L)	697
		Finished goods stock c/f	11,618
	136,273		136,273

Working notes:

1. material and in-process stock = 4,000 kg × £0·75 + £7,909 + £10,054 = £20,963
2. conversion cost = £18,800 + £30,100 + £14,390 = £63,290
3. residual variances:

	£	
residual variance	15,159	(For all processes)
abnormal process losses	17,083	(For all processes)
WIP damage written off	2,393	(For all processes)
	34,635	

4. finished goods stock = 500 units × £23·235 = £11,618
   Note that unit cost may be obtained from Table 1 as £124,655/5,365 = £23·235
5. Other values are taken directly from Tables 1 and 2

(b) The accounting system currently in use by EVCO plc records quantities and values in each of making, converting and finishing processes. This system records the inputs to each process, the transfers from one process to another, normal and abnormal losses and residual variances.

The use of 'backflush accounting' focuses on the output and then works backwards when allocating costs between cost of goods sold (or finished goods) and stock valuations. Backflush accounting will be seen as relevant where the overall process cycle time is short and levels of materials and WIP are low. Such conditions are likely to occur where a just-in-time approach to production and sales is in force. EVCO plc currently has a policy of holding constant levels of stocks and WIP. It also uses the standard process costing variance analysis as its control mechanism. A move to a backflush accounting system would require alternative performance indicators for the various aspects of production and sale, such as a set of non-financial indicators.

The backflush accounting system simplifies the accounting records by avoiding the need to trace the movement of materials and WIP through the production processes.

(c)

EVCO plc

Report to management team

Subject: performance measurement

(i) The accounting information for the period ended 30 April 1996 highlights a number of major problems as follows:

- deteriorating profit levels with an actual loss of £15,640 instead of a budget profit of £26,454

- reduction in sales volume of approximately 3·5%

- high levels of process losses as indicated by high abnormal losses written off

- high levels of losses to raw materials, WIP and finished goods

- high levels of residual process variances which probably indicate poor levels of productivity and high idle time

- likely customer dissatisfaction through high replacement of faulty units and late deliveries.

(ii) Customer dissatisfaction may be due to high levels of faulty goods and late deliveries which may be worsened by losses of finished goods before delivery. The following budget and actual figures apply:

	Budget	Actual
Free replacement (as percentage of sales delivered)	208/5208 = 4%	500/5335 = 9·4%
Late deliveries (as percentage of net sales)	500/5000 = 10%	773/4835 = 16%
Finished goods stock losses (as percentage of stock)	10/500 = 2%	30/500 = 6%

(Note: The units used in the above calculations are obtained from Table B values (£) using £23·235 as unit valuation and a price penalty reduction value of £1·50 per unit as appropriate.

e.g. Actual finished goods losses = £697/23·235 = 30 units

Budget late deliveries = £750/1·50 = 500 units).

(iii) A total quality management programme should help overcome the range of problems which currently exist. Total quality management should, for example, aim at:

- an environment of zero defects at minimum cost e.g. to overcome process losses

- delivery of a quality product to customers thus eliminating free replacements

- reduction in cycle times and the elimination of non-value added activities thus reducing stock levels/losses and avoiding late deliveries

- improved awareness of all personnel of the need for a 'quality culture' in the company in order to improve performance at all levels.

I shall be pleased to supply any further information on request.

A Person

Management Accountant

June 1996

---

4 (a) *Intangibility:* in a service business it is less likely that there will be a single measurable output object. In the bank example, the helpfulness of employees or the speed of response to enquiries may influence the customer perception of the output quality and quantity.

Heterogeneity: the standard of performance in providing the service may vary. This is particularly so where there is a high labour input as in the bank example. It may be difficult to compare the performance of employees through time or with each other. Efforts should be made to specify a standard of performance which should be aimed for in both tangible and intangible aspects of the service. For example reply to written queries within 48 hours or telephone call-back within one hour for awkward telephone queries.

Simultaneity: this refers to the production and consumption of a service being at the same time. There is no opportunity to check it before delivery to the customer. In the bank example this applies to the telephone queries. Responses to written queries could be checked, however, before being sent out.

Perishability: services cannot be stored. This causes problems where there is a fluctuation in demand. A surge in telephone enquiries may swamp the system. A surge in written queries could probably be overcome through overtime working or the employment of temporary staff.

(b) The existing system appears to have a number of problems:

- poor telephone response time and quality of response

- high backlog of written queries

- high staff turnover and low morale

- high level of overtime working.

The bank will wish to ensure that 'value for money' is being achieved in the delivery of the service to customers. Failure to respond in a timely and efficient manner is likely to lead to loss of existing customers and potential new customers.

The present work distribution into geographical area groups where each employee is expected to answer telephone queries and undertake written work on any topic is unlikely to produce a quality system.

It would be more appropriate to have teams of employees with each team responsible for a particular type of enquiry. Each team would be responsible for telephone and written responses in a specific area e.g. maturity value quotations. This should be effective in a range of ways including:

- team resources can be directed to telephone or written queries according to demand fluctuations

- team ethos can be cultivated in order to increase pride in work and to help achieve an overall high level of performance

- overtime requirements should be reduced through better work organisation

- staff turnover and associated costs should be reduced through the improved quality of work environment and team support

- customers should receive a quicker and more effective response to queries which should help the corporate image of the bank and its ability to retain or increase its market share.

5 (a) Standard costing involves the setting of standards at agreed levels of price and performance and the measurement of actual events against such standards in order to monitor performance. The variance analysis will measure changes in performance and price for sales, material, labour and overhead. A basic assumption is that the standards will apply over a time period during which they provide a suitable base against which to measure actual events.

A total quality environment adopts a different philosophy:

- it aims towards an environment of zero defects at minimum cost. This conflicts with the idea of standard costs which, for example, accept that a planned level of yield loss has been built into material standards

- it aims towards the elimination of waste, where waste is defined as anything other than the minimum essential amount of equipment, materials, space and worker time. Standard costs may be set at currently attainable levels of performance which build in an accepted allowance for 'waste'

- it aims at continuous improvement. The focus is on performance measures which illustrate a continuous trend of improvement rather than a 'steady state' standard performance which is accepted for a specific period

- it is an overall philosophy requiring awareness by all personnel of the quality requirements in providing the customer with products of agreed design specification. Standard costing tends to place control of each variance type with specific members of management and workforce. This view may cause conflicting decisions as to the best strategy for improvement.

(b) Standard costing will measure labour efficiency in terms of the ratio of output achieved: standard input. This measure focuses on quantity and does not address other issues of effectiveness. Effectiveness in a total quality context implies high quality with a focus on value added activities and essential support activities. Efficiency (in terms of output) may be achieved at a cost. In a total quality context such costs may be measured as internal or external failure costs which will not be identified in the standard cost variance measure.

In a standard cost system, individual labour task situations are used as a basis for efficiency measurement. In a total quality environment it is more likely that labour will viewed in multi-task teams who are responsible for the completion of a part of the production cycle. The team effectiveness is viewed in terms of measures other than output, including incidence of rework, defect levels at a subsequent stage in production, defects reported by the customer.

6   If group profit maximisation is to result from decisions made using transfer prices, the transfer prices should be set using the 'general rule' that transfer price = marginal cost + opportunity cost to the group. The information flow between divisions which will enable the general rule principle to be applied may be affected by the degree of autonomy that each division is allowed. Divisional autonomy implies that the management at each division is allowed to operate in an independent manner free from directives from group management. In this situation, divisional management are likely to operate at arms' length and simply quote the best price which they think the market will bear.

The Istana Division – Taman Division situation may be studied from a number of viewpoints:

(i)   Where Istana Division has an external market for its product (80% of its capacity), the transfer price should be set at market price in order to comply with the general rule. In this way any external supply available to Taman Division at less than the market price of Istana Division's product will increase group profit.

(ii)   It may be that there are some costs associated with external sales which are not incurred on inter-divisional business. For example less packaging may be required and delivery costs may be reduced. In such a situation, Istana Division should quote an adjusted market price which excludes the costs not relevant to inter-divisional business. In this way Istana Division will earn the same profit as it would from external sales and Taman Division will reject external supplier quotes which are in excess of the adjusted market price quoted by Istana Division.

(iii)   Istana Division has 20% spare capacity for which, it appears, no external market exists. It should offer to transfer output from the 20% spare capacity to Taman Division at marginal cost on the basis that zero opportunity cost to the group exists for this capacity. In this way Taman Division will reject any external supplier quotes in excess of the marginal cost of Istana Division.

(iv)   We are told that the external supplier can supply 75% of Taman Division's requirement. This is equivalent to 30% of the capacity of Istana Division. Remember that Istana Division has 20% spare capacity, which means that the residual 10% which the external supplier could provide represents external sales of Istana Division. It will be useful for Istana Division to indicate the quantities which it is willing to supply at different prices viz., 20% capacity at marginal cost and 10% capacity at adjusted market price. In this way Taman Division can evaluate the offer from the external source taking into account the possibility that the external source may require a higher price for a part order.

This marking scheme is given as a guide to markers in the context of the suggested answer. Scope is given to markers to award marks for alternative approaches to a question, including relevant comment, and where well reasoned conclusions are provided. This is particularly the case for essay based questions where there will often be more than one definitive solution.

		marks	marks
1 (a)	sales 2×0.5	1	
	direct material 2×1	2	
	direct labour – first six months	4	
	– second six months	6	
	variable overhead 2×0.5	1	
	DAFC 2×0.5	1	
	target return 2×0.5	1	
	decision	1	
		—	17
(b)	method (on merit)	2	
	correct figures	4	
		—	6
(c)	target costing/pricing explanation	3	
	specific action to improve	6	
	problems to be avoided	3	
	(allow up to 2 marks for presentation)	—	12
			35

			marks	marks
2	(a)	Table 1 comments:		
		ROI and RI short term	3	
		ROI and RI long term	1	
		NPV	2	
		Table 2 comments:		
		for change in contribution/hour impact on ROI, RI, NPV (on merit)	4	
			—	10
	(b)	(i) annual equivalent cash flow	2	
		imputed interest 2 × 0·5	1	
		depreciation 2 × 1	2	
		overall layout (incl. profit, RI)	2	
		ROI 2 × 0·5	1	
			—	8
		(ii) comments on merit		4
	(c)	calculation and comment		3
	(d)	(i) increase loss – level 1	2	
		increase profit – level 2	2	
			—	4
		(ii) ZBB explained (on merit)	4	
		Eastpark comment	2	
			—	6
				35

			marks	marks
3	(a)	input and output items in material and in-process account and finished goods account (10 × 1)		10
	(b)	backflush accounting principles compared to EVCO now	3	
		short time cycle	1	
		low stock and WIP levels	1	
			—	5
	(c)	(i) poor performance factors (6 × 1)	6	
		(ii) percentage indicators (6 × 1)	6	
		(iii) TQM features including use to EVCO (4 × 2)	8	
			—	20
				35

		marks	marks
4	(a) terms explained 3 × 1	3	
	examples 3 × 1	3	
	plus floating marks on merit for good quality answers	2	
		—	8
	(b) problems identified	3	
	advantages of team grouping	4	
		—	7
			15

5	(a) general comments	2	
	specific TQM v Standards differences (any 3) 3 × 2	6	
		—	8
	(b) std costing – efficiency linked to output etc	3	
	TQM – effectiveness, failure costs, etc	4	
	(overall allow marks on merit)	—	7
			15

6	general rule principles	3	
	different views of Istana/Taman situation (4 × 3)	12	
		—	15
			15

Module E – Professional Stage

Accounting and Audit Practice

(Scots)

June 1996

Question Paper:	
Time allowed	**3 hours**
This paper is divided into two sections	
Section A	TWO questions ONLY to be answered
Section B	BOTH questions are compulsory and MUST be answered

Section A – TWO questions ONLY to be attempted

1 The following information relates to the balance sheets of Ren plc, its subsidiary Sino plc, and an associated company Malic Ltd at 31 May 1996.

	Ren plc £000	Sino plc £000	Malic Ltd £000
Tangible Fixed assets	16,400	14,500	
Investments			5,000
Shares in Sino plc (at cost)	13,200		
Shares in Malic Ltd (at cost)	3,000		
	32,600	14,500	5,000
Current assets			
Stock	2,612	2,010	
Debtors	2,036	1,195	
Cash at bank and in hand	882	115	
	5,530	3,320	
Creditors: amounts falling due within one year	2,502	1,360	
Net Current Assets	3,028	1,960	
Total assets less current liabilities	35,628	16,460	
Creditors: amounts falling due after more than one year	5,350	1,470	
	30,278	14,990	
Capital and Reserves			
Ordinary £1 shares	20,000	8,000	5,000
7% £1 Preference shares		4,000	
Share premium account	4,950	350	
Profit and loss account	5,328	2,640	
	30,278	14,990	5,000

The following points are relevant to the preparation of the Ren plc group balance sheet:

(a) Ren plc owns 80% of the ordinary £1 shares and 30% of the 7% £1 preference shares of Sino plc.

    (i) The preference shares of Sino plc were originally issued on 1 June 1995 at par and are to be redeemed on 31 May 2005 at a premium of 10%.

    (ii) Ren plc paid £13·2 million for the ordinary £1 shares and the 7% £1 preference shares on 1 June 1995 when Sino plc's profit and loss account was £3 million (credit balance).

    (iii) The share premium account of Sino plc comprises the original premium on the issue of the ordinary shares.

    (iv) Any premium on the redemption of preference shares is to be dealt with, for the purposes of FRS 4, Capital Instruments, by using the straight line method. The premium has not been dealt with in the accounting records of Sino plc.

(b) The fair value of the net assets of Sino plc were not materially different from their book value at the time of its acquisition by Ren plc.

(c) Sino plc has already paid its dividends for the current financial year and no other dividends are proposed. The company paid an ordinary dividend of 1p per share and the 7% preference dividend. Ren plc has included the dividends received in its profit and loss account. The auditors of Ren plc observed that the payment of the dividends by Sino plc was out of pre acquisition profits and has contributed to a diminution in the value of the holding company's investment. They feel that Ren plc should account for the dividends accordingly.

(d) Sino plc sold an item of stock to Ren plc on 1 July 1995. Ren plc has treated this item correctly as plant and machinery in its financial statements. The item was sold at cost plus 20% and is shown in the fixed assets of Ren plc at £2·4 million. A full year's depreciation of 20% per annum has been charged on this amount in the financial statements of Ren plc. Ren plc has not fully paid the cost of the fixed asset to Sino plc. There is an amount of £500,000 outstanding.

(e) Ren plc bought 30% of the shares of Malic Ltd on 31 May 1996. Malic Ltd is an investment company whose only asset is a portfolio of investments with a book value of £5 million. The market value of these investments on 31 May 1996 was £9 million.

(f) Goodwill arising on acquisition is to be written off against the profit and loss account in the year of acquisition.

    [P.T.O.

Required:

(a) Prepare the consolidated balance sheet for the Ren Group plc as at 31 May 1996. (21 marks)

(b) Describe, with reasons, the different ways in which a dividend paid by a subsidiary out of pre-acquisition profits may be treated in the accounting records of the holding company.

(4 marks)

(25 marks)

2 The partnership firm of Damon and Hull was formed on 1 January 1995 and it was agreed that profits were to be shared 60% (Damon) to 40% (Hull). There were to be no partnership salaries and no interest paid on their capital accounts. No drawings were made by the partners. On 1 July 1995 they formed a limited company, DH Ltd, but did not keep separate accounting records for the partnership and limited company. All of the business transactions during the 18 month period, 1 January 1995 to 30 June 1996, had been recorded in a single set of accounting records. However, the accountant had been able to calculate the profit for the periods 1.1.95 to 30.6.95 and 1.7.95 to 30.6.96 but had not made the necessary capital adjustments. The following information has been extracted from the accounting records at 30.6.96.

	DR £	CR £
Capital Accounts at 1/1/95		
Damon		45,000
Hull		25,000
Net Profit before tax 1.1.95 to 30.6.95		16,500
Net Profit before tax and interest 1.7.95 to 30.6.96		56,000
£1 Ordinary shares		70,000
7% Debentures (repayable 1.7.2005)		15,000
Issue costs of debentures	1,000	
Stock and work-in-progress	37,000	
Debtors (including ACT recoverable)	45,500	
Debtors subject to financing arrangements	5,000	
Cash at bank and in hand	13,500	
Dividends paid on 1.1.96	10,000	
Creditors		51,000
Purchase consideration – DH Ltd	95,000	
Freehold property	30,000	
Depreciation on freehold property		1,000
Plant and machinery	30,000	
Depreciation on Plant & machinery		3,000
Vehicles	18,000	
Depreciation on vehicles		4,500
Loss on revaluation of net assets at 30.6.95	2,000	
	287,000	287,000

[P.T.O.

Additional Information

(a) The 7% debenture stock was issued on 1.7.95 and is repayable on 1.7.2005. The costs of issuing the debentures amounted to £1,000. The interest for the year to 30.6.96 had not been paid or accrued and the issue costs are to be dealt with on a straight line basis.

(b) DH Ltd sold some of its debtors to a factoring company on 30.6.96. The terms of the agreement were as follows. DH Ltd sold debtors of £33,000 to the factoring company. In exchange DH Ltd received £27,000 of which £23,000 is non returnable. The bad debts on the debtors sold are expected to be £1,000. £4,000 of the amount received is returnable depending on the performance of the debtors. The balance in the trial balance represents the amount of the debtors factored (£33,000) less the amount of cash received (£27,000) and the provision for bad debts (£1,000). DH Ltd has no obligation to repurchase any of the debtors sold and is not recognising any finance charges on this transaction until the next accounting period.

(c) The fair values of the net assets at 30.6.95 of the partnership were

	Fair value £
Freehold property	30,000
Plant and Machinery	30,000
Vehicles	18,000
Stock	16,000
Debtors	49,000
Cash at bank and in hand	25,000
Creditors	(83,500)
	84,500

The fair values were used to determine the purchase consideration and had been introduced into the accounting records at 30.6.95. Depreciation for the period 1.7.95 to 30.6.96 has been charged in the accounting records.

(d) When the limited company was formed it was agreed that the purchase consideration should be £95,000. The consideration was satisfied by the issue of the 70,000 £1 ordinary shares at par, £15,000 7% Debenture stock at par and the balance was paid in cash. The ordinary shares and debentures were divided between the partners in their profit sharing ratio. Expenses of dissolution amounting to £3,000 had been paid personally by Damon.

(e) The company proposes to pay a dividend of 4p per share on profits for the year.

(f) Any goodwill arising is to be amortised over five years on a straight line basis.

(g) A provision for corporation tax of £17,000 is to be made in the financial statements of DH Ltd. The ACT fraction to be used is 20/80.

Required:

(a) Prepare the Realisation and Capital accounts to record the cessation of the partnership of Damon and Hull at 30.6.95.

(6 marks)

(b) Prepare the opening balance sheet of DH Ltd at 1.7.95.   (4 marks)

(c) Prepare the balance sheet of DH Ltd at 30.6.96. (Your workings should show the calculation of the adjusted profit for the year ended 30.6.96).   (10 marks)

(d) Discuss the view that the financial statements sent to shareholders of small companies (such as DH Ltd) cannot show a true and fair view if they are exempt from certain disclosure requirements of the Companies Acts on the grounds of their size.

(5 marks)

(25 marks)

3 (a) Briefly describe **FIVE** key changes in financial reporting which were brought about by the introduction of FRS 3 'Reporting Financial Performance'. (5 marks)

(b) Explain how the profit or loss on the disposal of an asset is calculated under FRS 3 'Reporting Financial Performance' and why this method is used. (3 marks)

(c) Explain the criteria which determine

(i) whether an item is recognised in the financial statements

(ii) whether an item once recognised, appears in the profit and loss account or the statement of recognised gains and losses. (8 marks)

(d) On 1 January 1992 a company acquired a fixed asset for £25,000. It is to be depreciated at 20% on the reducing balance method. The company's policy is to revalue its assets every 2 years. On 31 December 1993 the asset was revalued to £18,000, its remaining useful life was determined to be 6 years and the depreciation method was changed to the straight line method.

On 31 December 1995 the asset was revalued to £8,000, but the useful life and depreciation method were not changed. This diminution in value was deemed to be permanent. On 1.4.96 the asset was sold for £8,500. Depreciation is not charged in the year of sale of an asset. The company draws up its financial statements to 31 December.

Required:

Show the annual effect (if any) of the above transactions for the period 1 January 1992 to 31 December 1996 on:

(i) the profit and loss account for the year

(ii) the profit and loss reserve brought forward in the balance sheet.

(iii) the revaluation reserve

(iv) the statement of recognised gains and losses. (9 marks)

(Students should assume that the company wishes to maximise its distributable profit for the period and wishes to be consistent with FRS 3.)

(25 marks)

Section B – BOTH questions are compulsory and MUST be attempted

4   Pot plc commenced work on three long term contracts during the financial year to 31 March 1996. The first contract with Shrigley plc commenced on 1 July 1995 and had a total sales value of £3·6 million. It was envisaged that the contract would run for two years and that the total expected costs would be £3 million. On 31 March 1996 Pot plc revised its estimate of the total expected costs to £3·1 million on the basis of the additional rectification costs of £100,000 incurred on the contract during the current financial year. An independent surveyor has estimated at 31 March 1996 that the contract is 40% complete. Pot plc has incurred costs up to 31 March 1996 of £1·5 million and has received payments on account of £1·2 million.

The second contract with Roast plc commenced on 1 October 1995 and was for a two year period. This contract was relatively small and had a total sales value of £60,000. The total expected costs were £48,000. A valuation has not been carried out by an independent surveyor as it was not required under the terms of the contract. The directors of the company estimated at 31 March 1996 that the contract was 30% complete. The costs incurred to date were £19,000 and the payments on account received were £21,000. A fixed asset which had cost £8,000 and had been purchased specifically for the project was considered to be obsolete as at 31 March 1996. The fixed asset was being depreciated on the straight line basis over the 2 year period of the contract assuming no residual value. The cost of depreciation to date was included in the amount of the costs incurred.

The third contract with Luck plc commenced on 1 November 1995 and was for $1^1/_2$ years. The total sales value of the contract was £2·4 million and the total expected costs were £2 million. Payments on account already received were £1 million and total costs incurred to date were £700,000. Pot plc had insisted on a large deposit from Luck plc because the companies had not traded together prior to the contract. The independent surveyor estimated that at 31 March 1996 the contract was 25% complete.

The company's policy is to calculate attributable profit by applying the degree of completion to estimated total profit and they are confident that their costings are accurate. The directors and auditors are satisfied that the contracts are sufficiently complete to accrue profit.

The company also has several short term contracts which are between 6 months and 9 months in duration. Some of these contracts fall into two accounting periods and were not completed as at 31 March 1996. The directors have decided to accrue profit earned to date on these contracts in the financial statements.

Required:

(a) Draft the profit and loss account and balance sheet extracts of Pot plc in respect of the three long term contracts for the year ending 31 March 1996. (Ignore the cash at bank balances.)   (11 marks)

(b) Discuss the acceptability of the accounting treatment by the directors of the contracts which run for between six months and nine months.   (4 marks)

(c) Describe the audit procedures necessary to verify long term contract balances.   (10 marks)

(d) Explain whether the auditors are likely to accept the company's policy of using an independent surveyor on some, but not all, of the contracts.   (5 marks)

(30 marks)

5   Broker Ltd is an investment brokers with a number of branches throughout the country. It deals with all aspects of the securities markets both on behalf of clients and on its own behalf. The employees of Broker Ltd are encouraged to use their own judgement and creativity in their dealings provided it increases the profitability of the company. The company has its own internal systems manual with which employees are encouraged to comply but often senior management override these controls. Additionally the directors often issue verbal amendments to the practices outlined in the manual.

One such amendment relates to its cash management policy. Each branch manager is encouraged to negotiate a bank overdraft limit at the local branch of a worldwide banking concern, and to take unauthorised overdrafts well beyond this limit. The branch managers are trained by the company in how to deal with the local bank manager and obtain the lowest possible charge for this practice.

Additionally the branch managers are encouraged to send out cheques to clients which will not be processed by the banks because of an irregularity on the cheque. For example, the cheque might be wrongly dated or not signed or purposefully defaced. This procedure improves the short term liquidity of the company. The branch managers are paid a basic salary plus an incentive payment based upon the interest earned on short term deposits and the profitability of the branch.

The bank has recently approached the company and is withdrawing its services because of the cash management policies of the company. The auditors have verbally raised the cash management practices with the audit committee who have promised to deal with the matter. The auditors have many years experience as auditors of other stockbroking companies but have never seen these practices before in these competitor companies. The directors stated that they have no knowledge of these practices and they also have accused the auditors of giving information about these cash management practices to their competitors.

Required:

(a) Explain how each of the elements of audit risk would be affected by the above information relating to Broker Ltd. (8 marks)

(b) Describe the audit procedures which should take place regarding the cash management practices of Broker Ltd. (7 marks)

(c) Explain the professional procedures which protect the confidentiality of a client's information when the audit firm also acts as auditor of a competitor company. (5 marks)

(20 marks)

End of Question Paper

Answers

1   **(a)**

Ren Group plc
Group Balance Sheet at 31 May 1996

	£000
Fixed Assets	
Tangible Assets	30,580
Investments	2,700
	33,280
Current Assets	
Stocks	4,622
Debtors	2,731
Cash at bank and in hand	997
	8,350
Creditors: amounts falling due within one year	3,362
Net Current Assets	4,988
Total Assets less Current Liabilities	38,268
Creditors: amounts falling due after more than one year	6,820
	31,448
Minority Interests	
Equity	2,110
Non Equity	2,828
	4,938
	26,510
Capital and Reserves	
Called up share capital	20,000
Share premium account	4,950
Profit and Loss account	1,560
Shareholders funds:	
Equity	26,510
	26,510

(a) *Workings – (£000)*

Treatment of Sino plc

Cost of Control

Cost of Shares	13,200	Ordinary shares	6,400
		Preference shares	1,200
		Share Premium	280
		Profit/loss account-Sino	2,400
		Profit/loss account-group	148
		Goodwill	2,772
	13,200		13,200

Profit/Loss Account – Sino plc

Premium on Redemption of preference Shares	40	Bal	2,640
Bal c/d	2,600		
	2,640		2,640
Cost of Control	2,400	Bal	2,600
Minority Int.	520	Profit/loss account-group	320
	2,920		2,920

Note premium on redemption of preference shares is $\dfrac{(10\%) \text{ of } 4000}{10 \text{ years}}$ i.e. 40

Minority Interest

Inter Co Profit	80	Ordinary Shares	1,600
		Preference Shares	2,800
		Premium on Redemption of pref Shares	28
Bal	4,938	Share Premium	70
		Profit & Loss a/c – Sino plc	520
	5,018		5,018

Profit/Loss Account – Group

Profit/Loss account	320	Bal	5,328
– Sino plc		Premium on redemption	
Cost of Control	148	of Pref Shares	12
Inter Co Profit (note d)	320	Deprn adj	80
Goodwill			
– Sino plc	2,772		
– Malic Ltd	300		
Bal	1,560		
	5,420		5,420

(b) *Share Premium – Sino plc*

Cost of Control	280	Bal	350
Minority Interest	70		
	350		350

(c) *Dividends paid*

	Total	Ren plc
Ordinary dividend (1%)	80	64
Preference dividend (7%)	280	84
	360	148

These dividends have been paid out of pre acquisition profits and therefore as they have contributed to the diminution in the value of the holding company's investment, they should be charged against the cost of that investment in the Cost of Control a/c.

(d) *Inter Company Stock/Fixed Asset*

Inter Company Profit: $\frac{20}{120}$ of £2,400 = £400

DR Minority Interest	80	
Group Profit/Loss	320	
CR Fixed Assets	400	

Depreciation Adjustment

Excess depreciation 20% of £400 = £80

DR Depreciation provision	80
CR Group Profit/Loss	80

(e) *Malic Ltd*

Cost of Shares	3,000
Fair value of investments acquired (30% of 9,000)	(2,700)
Goodwill	300

(f) *Equity and non equity interests*

Minority Interest

	Equity	Non Equity	
Ordinary Shares	1,600		
Preference shares		2,800	
Premium on Preference Shares		28	
Share Premium a/c	70		
Profit/Loss res.	520		
Inter Co Profit	(80)		
	2,110	2,828	4,938 TOTAL

Note: the shareholders funds of the group are all equity interests. The accrual of the premium on the preference shares is essentially equity income as would be an accrual of a preference dividend.

(b) Prior to FRS 6 a dividend paid out of pre-acquisition profits by a subsidiary was treated as a return of the capital paid to acquire the company and was not treated as realised profit in the hands of the holding company. Thus, it was applied to reduce the cost of the investment in the holding company's balance sheet.

An alternative view is that since accounting practice and the Companies Acts require provision to be made only for permanent diminution in the value of a fixed asset, provided that the investment will eventually recover the value which has been removed from it by the distribution, then it is unnecessaary to write it down and the dividend to the holding company may be distributed. This is on the assumption that the cost of the investment represents the fair value of the subsidiary.

This would allow holding companies to distribute all of the pre acquisition profits of a subsidiary provided that the subsidiary was going to earn the same amount in profits in the future.

FRS 6, Acquisitions and Mergers, gives some guidance on the matter by saying that a pre-acquisition dividend need not necessarily be applied as a reduction in the 'carrying value' of the investment in the subsidiary. Such a dividend should be applied to reduce the carrying value to the extent necessary to provide for any diminution in value. To the extent that this is not necessary, FRS 6 says that such an amount will be realised profit in the hands of the parent company.

2 (a)

Realisation Account

	£		£
Sundry net assets (84,500 + 2,000)	86,500	Purchase consideration	95,000
Expenses	3,000		
Profit – Damon	3,300		
Profit – Hull	2,200		
	95,000		95,000

Capital Accounts

	Damon £	Hull £		Damon £	Hull £
Ord Shares	42,000	28,000	Balance	45,000	25,000
Debentures	9,000	6,000	Expenses	3,000	
Cash	10,200		Profit	9,900	6,600
			Realisation a/c	3,300	2,200
			Cash		200
	61,200	34,000		61,200	34,000

Workings

Profit and Loss Account Damon and Hull

		£
(i)	Net profit for period 1.1.95 to 30.6.95	16,500
	Damon 60%	9,900
	Hull 40%	6,600
		16,500

Partnership Cash Account (extract)

		£		£
(ii)	Cash from DH Ltd	10,000		
	Cash from Hull	200	Cash to Damon	10,200
		10,200		10,200

(b)   *Balance Sheet at 1.7.95 D H Ltd*

	£
Freehold Property	30,000
Plant and Machinery	30,000
Vehicles	18,000
Tangible Fixed Assets	78,000
Intangible Assets (goodwill)	10,500
	88,500

Current Assets

Stock	16,000
Debtors	49,000
Cash	14,000
	79,000
Creditors – amounts due within 1 year	(83,500)
Net current assets	(4,500)
Total assets less current liabilities	84,000
Creditors: amounts due after 1 year	(14,000)
	70,000

Capital and Reserves

| £1 Ordinary Shares | 70,000 |

Working

(iii) Goodwill = Purchase consideration £95,000 – Fair Value of net assets £84,500 i.e. *£10,500*.

(iv) Cash = £25,000 – £11,000 i.e. balance from partnership less cash included in purchase consideration and issue costs.

(c)   *Balance Sheet of DH Ltd at 30.6.96*

	£
Freehold Property	29,000
Plant and Machinery	27,000
Vehicles	13,500
Tangible Fixed Assets	69,500
Intangible Assets	8,400
	77,900

Current Assets

Stock	37,000
Debtors	43,700
Debtors subject to financing arrangements	9,000
Cash	13,500
	103,200
Creditors – amounts falling due within one year	(74,050)
Net Current Assets	29,150
Total Assets less current liabilities	107,050
Creditors: amounts due after 1 year	(14,100)
	92,950

Capital and Reserves

Called up share capital – ordinary £1 shares	70,000
Profit/loss account	22,950
	92,950

Workings

	£
(v) Net Profit before taxation 1.7.95 to 30.6.96	56,000
Goodwill written off	(2,100)
Interest payable	(1,050)
Corporation tax	(17,000)
Issue costs	(100)
Dividends paid + proposed	(12,800)
	22,950

(vi) *Creditors: amounts falling due within one year*	£	£
Creditors per trial balance		51,000
Corporation tax provision	17,000	
less ACT recoverable (20/80 of £10,000)	(2,500)	14,500
ACT payable		700
Cash returnable to factor		4,000
Interest payable		1,050
Proposed dividend		2,800
		74,050

(vii) *Factored Debts*	£
Gross Amounts (33,000 – 1,000)	32,000
less Non returnable proceeds	23,000
	9,000

(viii) *Debtors*	£
	45,500
less ACT recoverable	(2,500)
plus ACT recoverable on proposed dividends	700
	43,700

(d) The financial statements of large and small companies have until recently been very similar. However, the introduction of exemptions from disclosure has altered this situation and has introduced certain problems. Accounting practice generally deals with three fundamental areas. These areas are recognition, measurement and disclosure. Small companies have to comply with the basic rules of recognition and measurement but no longer need to disclose as much information in their financial statements as large companies. The problem is that if large companies do not disclose certain information (e.g. their liability for corporation tax) then their accounts will probably not show a true and fair view. However, if small companies do not disclose this information then their accounts may show a true and fair view.

Thus, it appears that two sets of generally accepted accounting practice are developing with small companies only having to comply with a restricted set of rules. The truth and fairness of the financial statements of a small company was assured under the Companies Acts even if the directors take advantage of the statutory exemptions available to them.

However, there is now a problem developing whereby small companies no longer need to disclose basic information under the Companies Acts but do have to comply with complex disclosures under the Financial Reporting Standards. The financial statements of a small company may show a statutory 'true and fair view' but will appear inconsistent from the users viewpoint compared to large companies.

It is important to determine the purpose of a small company's financial statements and then the nature of the information required in those statements can be determined. The truth and fairness of small company financial statements should be linked to the accountability of the company. The needs of users should determine the nature of the financial statements and not an arbitrary size criteria.

3 **(a)** FRS 3 'Reporting Financial Performance' changed the reporting of financial performance as follows:

(i) the profit and loss account has been reshaped so as to highlight a number of important components of performance. For example the results of continuing and discontinuing operations.

(ii) the analysis between continuing operations, acquisitions and discontinued operations should be disclosed to the level of operating profit.

(iii) extraordinary items are effectively eliminated and earnings per share is calculated after extraordinary items.

(iv) all exceptional items should be included in the profit and loss account under the statutory format headings to which they relate. Three items in this category should be shown separately:

(a) profits/losses on the sale or termination of an operation.

(b) cost of a fundamental reorganisation or restructuring

(c) profits or losses on disposal of fixed assets

(v) a new primary financial statement is introduced in the form of a 'statement of total recognised gains and losses'. Additionally the standard requires a memorandum note of historical cost profit and losses, and a reconciliation of opening and closing totals of shareholders funds for the period.

(b) FRS 'Reporting Financial Performance' requires that the profit or loss on the disposal of an asset be calculated as the difference between the net sale proceeds and the net carrying amount, whether carried at historical cost (less any provisions made) or at valuation. The reason for this revised approach to determining the profit and loss on the disposal of an asset lies in the ASB's balance sheet approach to the recognition of gains and losses set out in its Statement of Principles. The ASB defines gains and losses as being increases and decreases in equity (other than dividends and new share issues). Consequently once an asset has been revalued in the balance sheet, any subsequent transactions must be based on this value.

(c) For an item to be recognised in the financial statements it must meet certain criteria. These criteria are that:

(i) the item must meet the definition of an element of the financial statements.

(ii) there is evidence that there has been a change in the assets or liabilities inherent in the item.

(iii) the item can be measured reliably.

Thus, before an item can appear in the profit and loss account, or statement of recognised gains and losses, it must meet the definition of a 'gain' or a 'loss'. (Additionally, for the profit and loss account it could meet the definition of a 'distribution'). Also a transaction or event must have occurred which has resulted in a gain or loss, and this transaction must be capable of measurement. Where a change in assets is not offset by an equal change in liabilities a gain or loss will result, (unless the change relates to the entity's owners).

Gains or losses should be recognised in the profit and loss account or in the statement of recognised gains and losses. Gains which are earned and realised are recognised in the profit and loss account whilst gains which are earned but not realised are recognised in the 'statement of recognised gains and losses'. The same gains and losses should not be recognised twice. A revaluation gain on a fixed asset should not be recognised a second time when the asset is sold. This latter point explains the logic of the definition set out in part (b) of the answer.

For a gain to be earned there must be no material event to be performed. For example, the performance under a contract must have been completed. For a gain to be realised, a transaction which is measurable must have occurred, or a 'capital' item (for example fixed asset or debenture) must have been sold/redeemed resulting in cash or cash equivalents, or a liability must have ceased to exist. Thus a statement of recognised gains and losses represents an alternative profit and loss account for those items which do not meet the above 'realisation' criteria.

(The ASB has recently issued a draft Statement of Principles which may alter the above criteria).

(d)

	Balance Sheet	Profit/Loss Account	Profit/Loss Reserve	Revaluation Reserve	Statement Of Recognised Gains & Losses
Year ended 31.12.92					
Cost	25,000				
Depreciation	(5,000)	(5,000)			
Carrying Value	20,000				
Year ended 31.12.93					
Cost	25,000				
Depreciation	(9,000)	(4,000)			
Carrying Value	16,000				
Revaluation Surplus	2,000			2,000	
Carrying Value	18,000				2,000
Year ended 31.12.94					
Valuation	18,000				
Depreciation	(3,000)	(3,000)	333 (note 1)	(333)	
Carrying Value	15,000			1,667	
Year ended 31.12.95					
Valuation	18,000				
Depreciation	(6,000)	(3,000)			
Carrying Value	12,000				
Revaluation loss	(4,000)	(4,000) (note 2)	1,667	(1,667)	
Carrying Value	8,000			–	

	P/L a/c	P/L Res	Revn Res	St of RGL
Year ended 31.12.96				
Valuation	8,000			
Sale Proceeds	8,500			
	———			
Profit on Sale	500	500		
	═══			

Notes

(1) If this amount were transferred to the profit and loss account it would contravene FRS 3 as the standard does not permit amounts previously reported in the statement of recognised gains and losses to pass through the profit and loss account.

(2) An alternative method would be to charge only part of the revaluation loss to the profit and loss account.

This method is inconsistent with the treatment of sales of revalued assets under FRS 3 but many companies use it because it is less stringent than the method used in the answer and because there is an absence of a definitive standard in the area.

The accounting entries would be	DR P/L a/c	2,333
	DR Revaluation Reserve	1,667
	CR Fixed Assets	4,000

Workings

Year Ended 31.12.94	£
Depreciation charged on revalued asset	3,000
Depreciation based on historical cost amount £16000 ÷ 6	2,667
	———
Transfer from Revaluation reserve to Profit and Loss Reserve	333
	———

4 (a)

Pot Plc

EXTRACT

Profit and Loss Account for the Year Ended 31 March 1996

	£000
Turnover	2,058
Cost of Sales	(1,820)
	———
Gross Profit on long-term contracts	238
	———

Balance Sheet as at 31 March 1996

Current Assets	£000
Stock	
Long term contract balances	202
Debtors	
Amounts recoverable on contracts	240
Current Liabilities	
Payments on account	(200)

Workings

(1)	Long term contract – Roast plc	£
	Net costs	19,000
	Additional	6,000
	write-off of	
	Fixed Asset	
		25,000
	less Cost of Sales	(20,000)
		5,000
	less debtors payments	(3,000)
	on account (21,000 – 18,000)	
		2,000

(2)	Long term contract – Luck plc	£000
	Net costs	700
	less Cost of sales	500
	Long term contract balance	200
	less payments on account	
	Debtors	600	
	Cash	(1,000)	(400)
	Current liability	(200)

(3)   *Profit and Loss Account for Year Ended 31 March 1996*

	£000 Contract with Shrigley plc	£000 Contract with Roast plc	£000 Contract with Luck plc	£000 Total
Turnover				
40% of £3·6m	1,440	(30% 18 of 60)	(25% 600 of 2·4m)	2,058
Cost of Sales				
40% of £3m	1,200	(30% 12 of 40)	(25% 500 of 2m)	1,712
Additional Costs	100 (1,300)	Fixed 8 Asset (20)	(500)	108 (1,820)
Profit (Loss) on long term contracts	140	(2)	100	238

(4)   *Balance Sheet as at 31 March 1996*

Current Assets

Stocks

Long term contract balances (£1·5m – £1·3m)	200	2 (Working 1)	202
Debtors			
Amounts recoverable on contracts (£1·44m–£1·2m)	240		240
Current Liabilities			
Payments on Account		(200) (Working 2)	(200)

(b) The definition of a long term contract in SSAP 9, 'Stocks and Long Term Contracts' says that a long term contract is one where 'the time taken substantially to complete the contract is such that the contract activity falls into different accounting periods. A contract that is required to be accounted for as long term . . . . will usually extend for a period exceeding one year . . . . Some contracts with a shorter duration than one year should be accounted for as long term contracts if they are sufficiently material . . . . that not to record turnover and attributable profit would lead to distortion'.

It would appear that the proposed accounting treatment by the directors is acceptable under SSAP 9. Since Pot plc is engaged in both long term contracts and short term contract, it is acceptable to apply the same accounting policy to both types of contract. However it is important that the accounting policy is applied on a consistent basis. The company should not adopt the completed contract method when it is expedient to do so. Criteria must be established for determining which contracts are to be accounted for under SSAP 9 as long term contracts and appropriate accounting policies established and applied consistently.

(c) The auditor would verify long term contract balances by undertaking the following procedures:

(i) Review the control environment for costs, payments on account and estimates

(ii) Analytical review of previous contracts (if any) looking at the outcome of contracts and the reliability of managements forecasts of profit. Also the analytical review can be used to identify problem areas, for example it can locate unusually large contracts, and evidence of disputes.

(iii) Review contracts themselves on an individual basis in order to gain knowledge of the terms of the contract. Also, interview company personnel in order to gain knowledge of individual contracts. This will enable the auditor to detect any inconsistencies between the forecast profit and the audit evidence available.

(iv) Ensure that the classification of contracts is in accordance with SSAP 9 and is consistently applied.

(v) Obtain a summary of all contract work in progress and the individual details of each contract.

(vi) Carry out compliance tests on the internal control system relating to long term contracts. The company's department responsible for estimating costs and revenues on contracts should be reviewed.

(vii) Carry out substantive tests on the individual contracts, work certified and payments on account.

(viii) Review basis and calculation of overhead apportionments to contracts and ensure that they are in accordance with SSAP 9.

(ix) Verify the treatment of interest on capital borrowed is in accordance with SSAP 9.

(x) Verify the reasonableness of any provisions for future losses.

(xi) Ensure profit is taken on contracts only where the outcome can be seen with reasonable certainty.

(xii) Verify the presentation and calculations of long term contract balances are as per SSAP 9 including verification of the basis of 'attributable profit'.

(xiii) Review the qualifications and status of the external surveyor responsible for estimating the work completed to date.

(xiv) visit the sites (if any) of long term contracts and observe the adequacy of stock counting and other asset verification procedures.

(xv) Review and verify any potential claims or contingent liabilities which may arise out of the long term contracts.

(d) SSAP 9 does not give any detailed guidance on who should have the responsibility for certifying the amount of work performed on the contract. On most contracts which are material, it is likely that the contract will specify that an independent surveyor should certify the amount of work performed. Thus the contracts where the directors are certifying the work completed are likely to be immaterial. However this may not always be the case and it is important that the auditors ensure that the principles applied by the directors are the same as those applied by the independent surveyor. These principles are as follows:

(i) The method of arriving at work certified should be reasonable with regard to the nature of the contract.

(ii) The method should be in accordance with methods adopted in the industry.

(iii) The method should be applied consistently between different contracts and over time.

If the directors apply consistently the same principles as the surveyor then the auditor will be able to accept the directors certification of work completed. However, the amount of work certified can be used by the directors to manipulate profits and therefore it is important for the auditors to closely review the basis of the directors certification.

5 (a) Audit risk means the risk that auditors may give an inappropriate audit opinion on the financial statements. The three components of audit risk (inherent risk, control risk and detection risk) will be affected by the nature of the operations of Broker Ltd.

The assessment of inherent risk will be affected by the following factors:

(i) The remuneration of the branch managers is based upon the interest earned on short term deposits and the profitability of the branch. The branch managers therefore have an incentive to inflate the interest and profits thus making the financial statements more prone to material misstatement.

(ii) The nature of the company's business. The company deals with all aspects of the securities markets. The business environment within which a stockbroker operates is quite complex and thus the inherent risk is increased in this type of business at both the financial statement level and at the account balance and class of transactions level.

(iii) Additionally the assets of the company are more susceptible to loss or misappropriation at the account balance and class of transactions level. The company is dealing in highly desirable assets, that is securities and cash, and thus the chance of misappropriation is greater.

(iv) The company deals in all aspects of the securities markets and via several branches. Thus it is likely that unusual and possibly complex transactions take place. If the managers can override controls then there may be transactions which may not be subject to the normal processing controls. For example managers may deal in financial derivatives which are high risk transactions.

(v) The integrity of the management must be questionable. The cash management policies of the company are at least unethical and possibly fraudulent. These practices might affect the integrity of the financial statements.

The assessment of control risk will be affected by the following factors:

(i) The corporate culture and control environment of Broker Ltd would affect adversely the level of control risk.

The laxity in the controls whereby management can override controls in the interests of profitability increases the likelihood that the internal controls would not be sufficient to prevent or detect material misstatements. (Additionally, directors can issue verbal amendments to practices within the company).

(ii) Also the managers are being trained in unethical practices in order to enhance profitability. A company that as part of its culture directs managers to send cheques to clients which cannot be processed will have an increased risk of possible control problems.

Detection risk

These factors will influence the nature, timing and extent of the auditors substantive audit procedures. The higher the assessments of inherent and control risk, the more audit evidence the auditors should obtain from the performance of substantive procedures in order to reduce detection risk to an acceptably low level. As a result, it is likely that the auditors will perform a larger proportion of their substantive procedures on the year end balances.

(b) The auditor should carry out the following audit procedures at the head office and branches regarding the cash management practices of the company.

(i) Review and test the bank reconciliation statements. The results of this test should confirm the unacceptable practices of the company regarding the issuing of cheques.

(ii) Review and test the procedures for controlling the supply and issue of cheque books, cheque authorisation and signing procedures, and the despatch of signed cheques.

(iii) Contact the bank and arrange for a sample of paid cheques to be returned to the auditor.

(iv) Review and test the procedure for dealing with paid cheques returned.

(v) Obtain direct from the bankers a bank certificate with details of the terms and conditions of any overdrafts.

(vi) Additionally enquire from the bank as to the reasons for the high level of returned cheques and for the reasons for the exceeding of the overdraft.

(vii) Obtain an explanation from the management of the company as to their cash management policies.

(viii) Obtain expert opinion as to the legality of the procedures being adopted by Broker Ltd.

(ix) Carry out an analytical review on the bank balances, interest paid, cheque returns and ask the client for explanations of any variances discovered.

(x) Report the audit finding to the audit committee and directors in writing. The potential effect on the financial statements of purposefully sending out incorrectly completed cheques and the potential going concern problems associated with and exceeding of the overdraft limit should be pointed out to the client.

(c) Auditors have a strict responsibility set out in the ethical guidance notes issued by the ACCA not to disclose confidential client information to third parties. Information confidential to a client acquired in the course of professional work should not be disclosed except where consent has been obtained from the client or where there is a legal right or duty to disclose. Anyone receiving confidential information in the course of their professional work should not use that information for personal advantage. Auditors are particularly aware of the rules regarding confidentiality because if the rules are broken the credibility of the profession and their own firm will come into question. When clients are in competition, auditors have to be particularly careful to ensure confidentiality. It is important that the same staff do not work on both assignments, and it must be stressed to these staff that they must not discuss the two clients affairs. The partners in charge of the two clients should be different and if possible a different office of the audit firm should deal with each client. Where it is extremely difficult to maintain absolute confidentiality in these circumstances, the audit firm should consider whether it can continue to act for both clients.

Question 1

		Marks
(a)	Cost of Control	5
	Profit/Loss account – Sino plc	3
	Minority Interest	3
	Group Profit/Loss account	3
	Share Premium account Sino plc	1
	Pre-acquisition dividend	2
	Inter company profit	2
	Inter company debt	1
	Associated company	2
	Equity v non equity interests	2
	Stock, cash, creditors more than 1 year	1
	Share Capital/Share Premium of group	1

Available	26
Maximum	21

(b)	Reduce cost of investment	1
	Return of capital	1
	Treat as realised profit	1
	Diminution in value of investment	1
	FRS 6 position	2

Available	6
Maximum	4
Total Available	32
Maximum	25

Question 2

(a)	Realisation account	3
	Capital Accounts	2
	Profit/Loss Account	1

Available	6
Maximum	6

			Marks
(b)	Goodwill		1
	Debentures		1
	Cash		1
	Other net assets		2
		Available	5
		Maximum	4
(c)	Intangible assets		1
	Tangible assets		1
	Current assets		1
	Creditors due in one year		4
	Creditors due more than one year		2
	Debtors/factored debts		4
		Available	13
		Maximum	10
(d)	Subjective assessment	Available/Maximum	5
		Total Available	29
		Maximum	25

Question 3

(a)	1 mark per point upto max		5
(b)	Definition of profit or loss		2
	Statement of Principles		1
		Available/Maximum	3
(c)	General recognition criteria		2
	'gain' or 'loss'		1
	Gains/losses recognised in either statement		1
	Gains earned and realised in p/l account		2
	Gains earned and not realised in statement of recognised gains and losses		2
	Same gains not recognised twice		1
	Definition of 'earned'		1
	Definition of realised		1
	Statement of recognised gains/losses – alternative profit/loss account		1
		Available	12
		Maximum	8

			Marks
(d)	Depreciation charge 1992/93/95/96		2
	1994		1
	Profit/Loss reserve 1994		2
	Revaluation reserve 1993		1
	Statement of recognised gains and losses		1
	Treatment of revaluation loss		2
	Profit on disposal		1
		Available	10
		Maximum	9
		Total Available	30
		Maximum	25

			Marks
Question 4			
(a)	Contract – Shrigley		4
	Roast		4
	Luck		4
		Available	12
		Maximum	11
(b)	Subjective assessment	Maximum	4
(c)	1 mark per point up to maximum		10

(d) No guidance   1
Material – independent surveyor   1
Consistent principles   1
Principles themselves   3
Manipulation   1

Available	7
Maximum	5
Available	33
Maximum	30

Question 5

(a) Definition of audit risk   1
Inherent risk element   5
Control risk element   3
Detection risk   2

Available	11
Maximum	8

(b) 1 mark per point up to maximum   7

(a) Definition of confidentiality   1
Credibility of profession   1
Staff not on same assignment   1
Non discussion of information   1
Different Partners   1
Different Offices   1
Consider whether continue in office   1

Available	7
Maximum	5
Available	25
Total	20

Module E – Professional Stage

Tax Planning
June 1996

Question Paper:	
Time allowed	3 hours
FOUR questions ONLY to be answered	
Tax rates and tables are on pages 70 to 72	

The following tax rates and allowances are to be used in answering the questions:

Income tax

		%
Lower rate	£1 – £3,200	20
Basic rate	£3,201 – £24,300	25
Higher rate	£24,301 and above	40

Personal allowances

	£
Personal allowance	3,525
Personal allowance – 65 – 74	4,630
Personal allowance – 75 and over	4,800
Married couple's allowance	1,720
Married couple's allowance – 65 – 74	2,995
Married couple's allowance – 75 and over	3,035
Income limit for age-related allowances	14,600
Additional personal allowance	1,720
Widow's bereavement allowance	1,720
Blind person's allowance	1,200

Car fuel scale charge

	Petrol £	Diesel £
Engine size		
1400cc or less	670	605
1401cc to 2000cc	850	605
2001cc and over	1,260	780

Mobile telephones

Cash equivalent of benefit	£200

Personal pension contribution limits

Age	Maximum percentage
Up to 35	17·5
36 – 45	20
46 – 50	25
51 – 55	30
56 – 60	35
61 or over	40

Subject to an earnings cap of £78,600

Capital allowances

	Percentage
Plant and machinery	
Writing-down allowance	25
Industrial buildings allowance	
Writing-down allowance	4
Agricultural buildings allowance	
Writing-down allowance	4

Corporation tax

Financial year	Full rate %	Small companies rate %	Taper relief fraction	ACT fraction	Upper limit £	Lower limit £
1990	34	25	9/400	25/75	1,000,000	200,000
1991	33	25	1/50	25/75	1,250,000	250,000
1992	33	25	1/50	25/75	1,250,000	250,000
1993	33	25	1/50	22·5/77·5	1,250,000	250,000
1994	33	25	1/50	20/80	1,500,000	300,000
1995	33	25	1/50	20/80	1,500,000	300,000

Marginal relief

$(M - P) \times I/P \times$ Tapering relief fraction

[P.T.O.

Value added tax

	£
Registration limit	46,000
Deregistration limit	44,000

Inheritance tax

£1 – £154,000	Nil
Excess	40%

Rates of interest

'Official rate' of interest: 10% (assumed)
Rate of interest on underpaid/overpaid tax: 10% (assumed)

Capital gains tax: *Retail Price Index*

March	1982	79·4
April	1983	84·3
June	1984	89·2
January	1986	96·2
April	1995	146·0
December	1995	148·0

Capital gains tax: *Annual exemption*

Individuals	£6,000

National Insurance (not contracted out rates)

		Rate	Lower limit £	Upper limit £
Class 1	Employee	10·0%[1]	58 p.w.	440 p.w.
	Employer	10·2%[2]	58 p.w.	—
Class 2		£5·75 per week		
Class 4		7·3%	6,640 p.a.	22,880 p.a.

[1] Earnings below £58 p.w. are exempt; where earnings exceed this limit the first £58 per week is taxable at a reduced rate of 2%.

[2] Reduced rates apply in respect of low earnings, as follows:

Band	
£ £	%
58 – 104·99	3
105 – 149·99	5
150 – 204·99	7

FOUR questions ONLY to be attempted

1   You are the tax adviser to the partnership of Smart and Sharp, a firm of management consultants. You should assume that today's date is 15 November 1995.

(a) There have been no changes to the constitution of the partnership for the past 10 years, but on 31 December 1995 a new partner is to be admitted. The recent tax adjusted Schedule D case II trading profits have been as follows:

	£
Year ended 31 December 1992	560,000
Year ended 31 December 1993	710,000
Year ended 31 December 1994	640,000

The partners are planning to incorporate the partnership's business on 31 December 1999. Forecast profits to this date are as follows:

	£
Year ended 31 December 1995	750,000
Year ended 31 December 1996	800,000
Year ended 31 December 1997	860,000
Year ended 31 December 1998	930,000
Year ended 31 December 1999	1,000,000

Required:

Calculate the partnership's Schedule D case II assessments for the years 1993–94 to 1999–2000 inclusive. You should assume that any favourable elections are made following the admission of the new partner on 31 December 1995, and that the partnership's business is incorporated on 31 December 1999. (10 marks)

(b) The partners would like advice as to whether or not it would be beneficial to incorporate the partnership's business when the new partner is admitted on 31 December 1995, rather than on 31 December 1999. They are concerned that the current level of profits of £750,000 may not be high enough for incorporation to be beneficial.

Following the admission of the new partner, the partnership will consist of five partners who will share profits equally. Upon incorporation, the partnership's business will be transferred to a new company, Smash Ltd. The five partners will all become directors of Smash Ltd, and would each receive directors remuneration of £125,000 p.a. Each of the five partners has sufficient investment income to utilise their personal allowances and basic rate income tax bands.

Required:

Advise the partners as to whether or not it would be beneficial for the partnership's business to be incorporated on 31 December 1995 rather than on 31 December 1999. Your advice should be based upon the following calculations:

(i) Assuming that the partnership's business is incorporated on 31 December 1995, calculate the Schedule D case II assessments of the partnership for 1993–94 to 1995–96, and the profits chargeable to corporation tax of Smash Ltd for the years ended 31 December 1996 to 1999. (3 marks)

(ii) Basing your answer solely on the current level of profits of £750,000, calculate (1) the annual tax liability of the five partners if the partnership *is not* incorporated, and (2) the annual tax liability of Smash Ltd and its directors if the partnership *is* incorporated.

Your answer should *take into account* the implications of NIC, and should use the tax rates for 1995–96. The figure for profits of £750,000 is *before* the deduction of directors remuneration.

(8 marks)

(c) The partners have asked for your advice regarding the CGT and IHT implications of incorporating the partnership's business.

Required:

Draft a reply to the partners. (4 marks)

(25 marks)

2 Albert Bone, a widower aged 64, died on 31 March 1996. The main beneficiary under the terms of Albert's will is his son Harold, aged 37. At the date of his death Albert owned the following assets:

(1) 76,000 £1 ordinary shares in Hercules plc. On 31 March 1996 the shares were quoted at 139 – 147, with bargains on that day of 137, 141 and 143.

(2) Building society deposits of £115,900.

(3) A life assurance policy on his own life. Immediately prior to the date of Albert's death, the policy had an open market value of £42,000. Proceeds of £55,000 were received following his death.

Albert was a beneficiary of two trusts:

(1) Under the terms of the first trust, Albert was entitled to receive all of the trust income. The trust owned 50,000 units in the Eureka unit trust, which was quoted at 90 – 94 on 31 March 1996. Accrued distributable income at 31 March 1996 was £800 (net).

(2) Under the terms of the second trust, Albert was entitled to receive the income at the discretion of the trustees. The trust's assets were valued at £95,000 on 31 March 1996.

Until 15 March 1987, Albert owned his main residence. On that date, he had made a gift of the property to Harold. Albert continued to live in the house with Harold, rent free, until the date of his death. On 15 March 1987 the property was valued at £65,000, and on 31 March 1996 it was valued at £180,000.

Albert has also made the following gifts during his lifetime:

(1) On 3 December 1988, he made a gift of £92,000 into a discretionary trust.

(2) On 18 October 1991, he made a gift of £24,500 to a granddaughter as a wedding gift.

(3) On 20 April 1992, he made a gift of ordinary shares (a 12% holding) in an unquoted trading company, into a discretionary trust. The shareholding was valued at £190,000, and had been owned for 10 years. The trust still owned the shares at 31 March 1996.

Any inheritance tax arising from the above gifts was paid by Albert.

At the date of his death, Albert owed £900 in respect of credit card debts, and he had also verbally promised to pay the £750 hospital bill of a neighbour. Albert's funeral expenses came to £1,200.

Under the terms of his will, Albert left specific gifts to his grandchildren totalling £40,000. The residue of his estate was left to Harold.

Required:

(a) Calculate the IHT that will be payable as a result of Albert's death. Your answer should show who is liable for the tax, and by what date. You should also include an explanation as to your treatment of Albert's main residence, and a calculation of the amount of the inheritance that Harold will receive.

You should ignore Albert's income tax liability for 1995–96, and should assume that the tax rates and allowances for 1995–96 apply throughout. (17 marks)

(b) Harold is to make a gift of some of his inheritance to his son, aged 8, so as to utilise his son's personal allowance. Advise Harold of whether or not such a gift would be effective for income tax purposes. Your answer should include any tax planning advice that you consider to be appropriate. (4 marks)

(c) Harold plans to invest the balance of his inheritance so as to achieve capital growth, since he already has sufficient income. He will require the capital in five years time when he is to purchase a new house. Briefly advise Harold of investments that would be appropriate for such an investment strategy. (4 marks)

(25 marks)

3 Techno plc is a rapidly expanding quoted company involved in management consultancy. The company is looking at ways of both motivating and retaining its 10 directors and 70 key personnel, of which several have recently been lost to competitors. The company has 400 other full-time employees, of whom 120 have joined the company during the past two years. One of the directors, Martin Thatch, owns 35% of the ordinary share capital of Techno plc. The other nine directors are 1% shareholders. None of the directors are connected to each other. The average remuneration of the directors and the key personnel is £100,000 p.a. and £40,000 p.a. respectively.

The proposals under consideration are as follows:

(1) Setting up a profit related pay scheme whereby directors and key personnel would be paid an annual bonus based on the increase in profit made by Techno plc compared to the previous year. It is likely that payments of up to £15,000 p.a. would be payable under the scheme.

(2) Setting up a profit sharing scheme whereby directors and key personnel would receive fully paid up ordinary shares in Techno plc free of charge each year. Techno plc would set up a trust to run the scheme, with the trust purchasing the shares required through the Stock Exchange, using funds provided by Techno plc.

(3) Providing each of the directors and key personnel with a new 2400cc petrol powered company motor car. The list price of each motor car is £27,500. In addition, each motor car will be fitted with a mobile telephone costing £500, and other optional accessories costing £2,000. Techno plc will also pay for private petrol, private telephone calls, and will provide free car parking spaces near its offices. The car parking spaces will be rented by Techno plc at a cost of £350 p.a. each. The motor cars will be driven between 5,000 and 10,000 miles on business each year.

(4) Providing each of the directors and key personnel with an interest free loan of £25,000. This loan will be written off in two years time, provided that the director or the key person is still employed by Techno plc at that date. The loan will be immediately repayable should a director or key person resign from Techno plc's employ.

(5) Setting up a share option scheme whereby directors and key personnel would receive options to purchase fully paid up ordinary shares in Techno plc at their present value. The options would be provided free, and would be exercisable in five years time.

Techno plc's ordinary shares are presently quoted at £1·00 each, and are likely to be worth £4·00 each in five years time. Techno plc is a close company.

Required:

(a) Explain the income tax, CGT and NIC implications for the directors and key personnel in respect of each of the five proposals. You should ignore the implications of VAT, and should assume that Inland Revenue approval, where applicable, *is not obtained* in respect of any of the proposals. (13 marks)

(b) (i) *Briefly* state the conditions that must be met in order for the profit related pay scheme (proposal one) and the profit sharing scheme (proposal two) to obtain Inland Revenue approval. Your answer should indicate whether or not the proposed schemes will qualify for approval.

You are not expected to discuss share option schemes or employee share ownership plans (ESOPs). (7 marks)

(ii) Advise the directors and key personnel of the potential tax saving if Inland Revenue approval *is obtained* for the profit related pay scheme and the profit sharing scheme. (5 marks)

(25 marks)

4 Hydra Ltd has owned 90% of the ordinary share capital of Boa Ltd and 80% of the ordinary share capital of Cobra Ltd since 1985. Cobra Ltd acquired 80% of the ordinary share capital of Mamba Ltd on 1 April 1995, the date of that company's incorporation. All of the companies are involved in the construction industry. The results of each company for the year ended 31 March 1996 are as follows:

	Tax adjusted Schedule D1 Profit/(loss) £	Capital gain/ (loss) £	Debenture interest paid £	Dividends paid £
Hydra Ltd	(45,000)	130,000	(20,000)	(55,000)
Boa Ltd	120,000	(15,000)	—	—
Cobra Ltd	85,000	—	—	(100,000)
Mamba Ltd	(12,000)	8,000	—	—

Hydra Ltd's capital gain arose from the sale of a factory for £350,000. As at 31 March 1995 the company had unused trading losses of £15,000, and surplus ACT of £18,000. Boa Ltd purchased a new office building on 1 May 1996 for £280,000. Cobra Ltd had surplus ACT of £12,000 as at 31 March 1995. Mamba Ltd's capital gain arose from the disposal of an investment.

A group income election in respect of dividends was in force throughout the year.

Required:

(a) Calculate the mainstream corporation tax liability for each of the four companies in the Hydra Ltd group for the year ended 31 March 1996. Your answer should include an explanation of your treatment of the trading losses of Hydra Ltd and Mamba Ltd, and the ACT of Hydra Ltd and Cobra Ltd. You should assume that reliefs are claimed in the most favourable manner. (18 marks)

(b) (i) Explain why it would probably be beneficial to transfer the 80% shareholding in Mamba Ltd from Cobra Ltd to Hydra Ltd.

(3 marks)

(ii) Hydra Ltd, Boa Ltd and Cobra Ltd all make standard rated sales, and are registered as a group for VAT purposes. The sales of Mamba Ltd are exempt. Briefly discuss the factors that would have to be considered when deciding if Mamba Ltd should be included in the group VAT registration. (4 marks)

(25 marks)

5 You are the tax adviser to Harry Chan, aged 43. Harry resigned from his position of sales manager with UTC Ltd, an *unquoted* trading company, on 31 March 1995. He had been employed at a salary of £45,000 p.a. On 15 April 1995 Harry sold 80,000 of the 100,000 £1 ordinary shares (a 1% holding) that he held in UTC Ltd for £3·35 per share. Harry originally acquired 25,000 shares at par on 15 June 1981, the date of UTC Ltd's incorporation. On 26 January 1986 UTC Ltd made a 3 for 1 rights issue at £5·00 per share, which Harry took up in full. The market value of UTC Ltd's shares at 31 March 1982 was £1·25 per share. The shares in UTC Ltd were the only chargeable asset that Harry held on 31 March 1982.

Harry used the proceeds from the disposal of his shareholding to purchase an existing business on 1 June 1995. The business is that of selling musical instruments, and Harry has run this as a sole trader. Accounts have been prepared for the 10 month period to 5 April 1996, and the results showed a marked decline compared to the results of the previous owner for the year ended 31 May 1995. The results are as follows:

	Previous owner Year ended 31 May 1995 £	Harry Chan Period ended 5 April 1996 £
Sales – Cash	300,000	200,000
– Credit	60,000	50,000
Gross profit	150,000	75,000
Net profit	108,000	40,000

Harry's accounts were submitted to the Inland Revenue on 1 May 1996. His tax adjusted Schedule D case I profit was the same as the net profit of £40,000. The Inland Revenue proceeded to carry out an investigation into Harry's accounts, and have stated that they consider the sales shown in the accounts to be understated by £50,000. On 1 July 1996 the Inland Revenue issued an estimated assessment for 1995–96 showing a Schedule D case I profit of £90,000. The assessment was appealed against on 15 July 1996, and an application was made at the same time to postpone £20,000 of the income tax liability. The Inland Revenue agreed to this postponement on 31 July 1996, and the income tax not postponed was paid by Harry on 22 October 1996.

Harry is single, and has no other income or outgoings.

Required:

(a) (i) State the likely reasons why the Inland Revenue have investigated Harry's accounts for the period ended 5 April 1996. (3 marks)

   (ii) State possible criteria that Harry could put forward in order to justify his profits of £40,000 for the period ended 5 April 1996. (2 marks)

(b) Assuming that Harry loses his appeal:

   (i) Calculate the interest on overdue tax that Harry will be charged in respect of his 1995–96 income tax liability.

   You should assume that the original assessment of Schedule D case I profit of £90,000 for 1995–96 becomes final on 31 December 1996, that Harry pays the income tax liability postponed of £20,000 on 10 January 1997, and that the Inland Revenue *do not* charge penalty interest under s.88 TMA 1970. You should *ignore* the implications of NIC and VAT. (7 marks)

   (ii) State the maximum amount of penalty that the Inland Revenue can charge Harry, and briefly advise him of the factors that will be taken into account in deciding if this maximum amount should be mitigated. (2 marks)

(c) (i) Calculate the capital loss that will arise from Harry's disposal of his 80,000 shares in UTC Ltd. (4 marks)

   (ii) Advise Harry as to the most beneficial way of utilising his capital loss. Your answer should cover the possibility of Harry either winning or losing his appeal against the assessment for 1995–96. (7 marks)

(25 marks)

6   On 31 December 1995 Muriel Grand, aged 52, made a gift of a house in London to her brother Bertie, aged 53. Muriel had bought the house on 1 April 1983 for £60,000. Surplus land adjoining the house was sold for £24,000 to a neighbour in June 1984, at which date the market value of the property retained was £72,000. The market value at 31 December 1995 has been agreed by the Inland Revenue as £320,000. Muriel occupied the house as her main residence until 30 September 1990, and then moved in to another house that she owned in Glasgow. Muriel elected for the house in Glasgow to be treated as her main residence from 1 January 1992 onwards. From 1 January 1985 to 30 September 1990 Muriel used 20% of the house exclusively for business purposes.

Bertie is to rent out the house in London, either unfurnished or as furnished holiday accommodation. In either case, the roof of the house must be repaired at a cost of £24,000 before it will be possible to let the house. The roof was badly damaged by a gale on 5 December 1995. If the house is let unfurnished, then Bertie will have to decorate it at a cost of £3,500. The forecast rental income is £28,000 p.a. If the house is let as furnished holiday accommodation, then the house will be converted into two separate units at a cost of £41,000. The total cost of furnishing the two units will be £9,000. This expenditure will be financed by a £50,000 bank loan at an interest rate of 12% p.a. The total forecast rental income is £45,000 p.a., although 22·5% of this will be deducted by the letting agency. Other running costs, such as cleaning, will amount to £3,500 p.a. in total.

Bertie plans to sell the house when he retires aged 60, and anticipates making a substantial capital gain. Both Muriel and Bertie are 40% taxpayers. Muriel has a portfolio of investments valued in excess of £1 million, and has already utilised her CGT annual exemption for 1995–96.

Required:

(a) Calculate the CGT liability that will arise from Muriel's gift of the house in London to Bertie. (4 marks)

(b) Advise Muriel as to how it would be possible to roll-over the gain on the house in London by making an investment in unquoted trading companies

Your answer should cover re-investment relief, the enterprise investment scheme and venture capital trusts, and you should describe the other tax implications of making such an investment. (8 marks)

(c) Advise Bertie of the tax implications of letting out the house in London either (i) unfurnished, or (ii) as furnished holiday accommodation. Your answer should include details of the tax advantages of letting the house as furnished holiday accommodation. (13 marks)

(25 marks)

End of Question Paper

Answers

1 (a) If a continuation election under s.113(2) ICTA 1988 is made by 31 December 1997, signed by all the partners old and new, the partnership's assessments will be as follows:

	£	£
1993–94 (PYB – year ended 31.12.92)		560,000
1994–95 (PYB – year ended 31.12.93)		710,000
1995–96 (PYB – year ended 31.12.94)		640,000
1996–97 (Transitional year) (750,000 + 800,000)/2		775,000
1997–98 (CYB – year ended 31.12.97)		860,000
1998–99 (CYB – year ended 31.12.98)		930,000
1999–2000 (1.1.99 to 31.12.99)	1,000,000	
Less: Transitional relief		
860,000 × 3/12	215,000	
		785,000
Total assessments		5,260,000

If no continuation election is made, the partnership's assessments will be as follows:

	£	£
Old partnership		
1993–94 (Actual 6.4.93 to 5.4.94)		
710,000 × 9/12	532,500	
640,000 × 3/12	160,000	
		692,500
1994–95 (Actual 6.4.94 to 5.4.95)		
640,000 × 9/12	480,000	
750,000 × 3/12	187,500	
		667,500
1995–96 (Actual 6.4.95 to 31.12.95)		
750,000 × 9/12		562,500

	£	£

New partnership

1995–96 (Actual 1.1.96 to 5.4.96)

800,000 × 3/12		200,000
1996–97 (CYB – year ended 31.12.96)		800,000
1997–98 (CYB – year ended 31.12.97)		860,000
1998–99 (CYB – year ended 31.12.98)		930,000
1999–2000 (1.1.99 to 31.12.99)	1,000,000	
Less: Overlap relief		
800,000 × 3/12	200,000	
		800,000
Total assessments		5,512,500

The Inland Revenue will apply s.63 ICTA 1988 to have 1993–94 and 1994–95 assessed on an actual basis, as this results in additional assessable profits of £90,000 ((692,500 + 667,500) – (560,000 + 710,000)).

The partners would be advised to make a continuation election as this reduces the total assessable profits by £252,500 (5,512,500 – 5,260,000).

(b) (i) If the partnership's business is incorporated on 31 December 1995, the assessable profits of the partnership and Smash Ltd will equate to the profits that would have been assessed on the partnership if its business was incorporated on 31 December 1999, and a continuation election was *not* made under s.113(2) ICTA 1988.

Assessments will therefore be as follows:

	£
Partnership	
1993–94 (As previous)	692,500
1994–95 (As previous)	667,500
1995–96 (As previous)	562,500
Smash Ltd	
Year ended 31.12.96	800,000
Year ended 31.12.97	860,000
Year ended 31.12.98	930,000
Year ended 31.12.99	1,000,000
Total assessments	5,512,500

Total assessable profits are therefore increased by £252,500.

(ii) *Tax liability of partners*

The annual tax liability of each of the five partners will be as follows:

	£
Schedule D case II (750,000/5)	150,000
Class 4 NIC relief (1,186 × 50%)	593
Taxable income	149,407

	£
Income tax at 40%	59,763
Class 2 NIC (5·75 × 52)	299
Class 4 NIC ((22,880 – 6,640) at 7·3%)	1,186
	61,248

The total annual tax liability of the five partners will be £306,240 (61,248 × 5).

Tax liability of Smash Ltd
The annual tax liability of Smash Ltd will be as follows:

	£	£
Trading profit		750,000
Directors remuneration (125,000 × 5)	625,000	
Employers class 1 NIC (625,000 at 10·2%)	63,750	
		688,750
PCTCT		61,250

	£
Corporation tax at 25%	15,312
Employers class 1 NIC	63,750
	79,062

Tax liability of directors
The annual tax liability of each director will be as follows:

	£	£
Taxable income – Schedule E		125,000
Income tax at 40%		50,000
Employees class 1 NIC		
58 × 52 at 2%	60	
382 × 52 at 10%	1,986	
		2,046
		52,046

The total annual tax liability of Smash Ltd and the five directors will be £339,292 (79,062 + (52,046 × 5)). This is an increase of £33,052 (339,292 – 306,240) compared to the total annual tax liability of the five partners.

Conclusion
Since incorporating the partnership's business on 31 December 1995 rather than on 31 December 1999 will result in both an increase of assessable profits, and (based on the current level of profits) an increase in the overall annual tax liability, incorporation on this date does not appear to be beneficial.

(c) *CGT implications*
The incorporation of the partnership's business will be a disposal for CGT purposes. Provided that the disposal is in return for shares in Smash Ltd, any gains arising from the disposal of chargeable business assets can be held over against the base cost of the shares received. For this relief to apply, the partnership's business must be transferred as a going concern, and all the assets of the partnership's business (excluding cash) must be transferred.

IHT implications
At present, were they to die, the four existing partners would be entitled to BPR at the rate of 100% in respect of their partnership share. The new partner will not be entitled to BPR until he or she has been a partner for two years. Following the incorporation of the partnership's business, most of, if not all of, the five partners will become minority shareholders of 25% or less in Smash Ltd, which will presumably be an unquoted company. The rate of BPR will therefore be reduced to 50%.

2　(a)　*Lifetime transfers of value*

15 March 1987 – The gift of the main residence is a PET. As this is more than seven years before the date of death, no IHT will be due. However, Albert has continued to live rent free in the property until the date of his death. The gift will therefore be classified as a gift with reservation, and the main residence will be included in Albert's estate at its value on 31 March 1996. There is no double charge to tax, as the PET does not become chargeable.

	£	£
3 December 1988		
Value transferred		92,000
Annual exemptions 1988–89	3,000	
1987–88	3,000	
	———	6,000
Chargeable transfer		86,000
IHT liability 86,000 at nil %		Nil
18 October 1991		
Value transferred		24,500
Marriage exemption	2,500	
Annual exemptions 1991–92	3,000	
1990–91	3,000	
	———	8,500
Potentially exempt transfer		16,000
20 April 1992		
Value transferred		190,000
Business property relief – 50%		95,000
		95,000
Annual exemption 1992–93		3,000
Chargeable transfer		92,000
IHT liability 154,000 – 86,000 = 68,000 at nil %		Nil
92,000 – 68,000 = 24,000 × 20/80		6,000
		6,000

As a result of Albert's death on 31 March 1996, additional IHT will be due. The revised cumulative total as a result of the PET on 18 October 1991 becoming chargeable is £102,000 (86,000 + 16,000).

	£
Gross transfer (92,000 + 6,000)	98,000

	£
IHT liability 154,000 – 102,000 = 52,000 at nil %	Nil
98,000 – 52,000 = 46,000 at 40%	18,400
Tapering relief 18,400 at 20 %	3,680
	14,720
IHT paid	6,000
	8,720

The additional IHT liability of £8,720 will be payable by the discretionary trust on 30 September 1996.

Alternatively, as the property consists of a shareholding of at least 10% in an unquoted company, the trust could pay the IHT liability in 10 equal instalments commencing on 30 September 1996.

Estate at death – 31 March 1996
The chargeable transfer on 3 December 1988 is more than seven years before the date of death, and will therefore drop out of the cumulative total. The revised cumulative total is £114,000 (16,000 + 98,000).

	£	£
Free estate		
Personalty		
Ordinary shares in Hercules plc		
76,000 at 140p ((137 + 143)/2)		106,400
Building society deposits		115,900
Life assurance policy		55,000
Accrued trust income		800
		278,100
Credit card debts	900	
Funeral expenses	1,200	
		2,100
Net free estate		276,000

	£	£
Settled property		
Interest in possession 50,000 at 90p	45,000	
Accrued income (800 × 100/80)	1,000	
	———	44,000
Gift with reservation		180,000
Chargeable estate		500,000
IHT liability 154,000 – 114,000 = 40,000 at nil %		Nil
500,000 – 40,000 = 460,000 at 40%		184,000
		———
		184,000

The verbal promise by Albert to pay his neighbour's hospital bill is unlikely to be deductible, as it has not been incurred for full consideration.

Rate of IHT on estate = 36·8% (184,000/500,000 × 100)

IHT of £101,568 (276,000 at 36·8%) will be due from the estate. This will be payable by the executors of Albert's estate on the earlier of 30 September 1996 or the delivery of their account. Harold will inherit £134,432 (276,000 – 40,000 – 101,568), since specific gifts of UK property do not normally carry their own tax.

IHT of £16,192 (44,000 at 36·8%) will be due from the interest in possession trust, and IHT of £66,240 (180,000 at 36·8%) will be due from Harold in respect of the gift with reservation. It will be possible for him to pay this IHT liability in 10 equal instalments commencing on 30 September 1996.

(b) Where a parent transfers capital to an unmarried child who is under 18, then the income therefrom continues to be treated as that of the parent. There is a *de minimis* limit where the income does not exceed £100. The rule also applies if a parent makes a settlement in favour of the child.

Harold should therefore arrange for the terms of Albert's will to be varied before 31 March 1998 so that the capital passes direct to his son. The variation is made by a deed of variation (or deed of family arrangement), it must be in writing, and must be signed by all of the beneficiaries under the will. The variation will not affect the IHT liability arising on Albert's estate.

(c) Harold would be advised to keep some of his funds in high interest accounts with banks or building societies, or in a money market fund, with interest being reinvested. A TESSA would be suitable, as would National Savings Certificates, since in both cases interest is normally accumulated over five years, and is tax-free.

Unit trusts and investment trusts offer a number of options for capital growth. Alternatively, Harold could invest directly in equity shares, although such a strategy would carry more risk. These investments could probably be made by way of a personal equity plan, but this would probably only be beneficial if Harold was otherwise utilising his CGT annual exemption. Short-dated low-coupon gilts and single premium bonds are other possible investments.

Since Harold requires the capital in five years time, most pension and life assurance based investments are unlikely to be suitable. Harold might consider investing some of his capital in unquoted companies by way of, for example, a venture capital trust, but such an investment may well carry too much risk for him.

3   (a)   The directors and key personnel earn over £8,500 p.a., and are therefore P11D employees.

Profit related pay (PRP) scheme

The payments would be treated as additional emoluments of the directors and key personnel, and will be assessable as normal under Schedule E on the receipts basis. Income tax will be due at the rate of 40%. There will be no further employees class 1 NIC liability as all directors and key personnel are already earning in excess of the upper limit of £22,880 (52 × £440). There will be no CGT implications.

Profit sharing scheme

The directors and key personnel will be assessed under Schedule E on the difference between the market value of the shares issued to them, and the amount paid for them (which in this case is nil). The assessment will therefore be £1·00 for each share allocated. There are no NIC implications. A CGT liability will arise when the shares are subsequently sold, with the shares having a base cost of £1·00 each.

Company motor cars

The directors and key personnel will be assessed under Schedule E on the benefit of the motor cars. In each case, the benefit will be £6,883 (27,500 + 2,000 = 29,500 × 35% × 2/3). The value of any optional accessory costing less than £100 would be excluded from the price of the motor car if it was fitted after the date of provision. The provision of mobile telephones will give rise to a separate benefit of £200 p.a., unless there is no private use. The provision of private petrol will give rise to a fuel benefit of £1,260. The provision of a free parking space near the place of work does not give rise to a benefit. There are no NIC implications.

Beneficial loans

Each director and key person will be assessed under Schedule E on the difference between the interest paid on the loan and the official rate of interest. The annual benefit will therefore be £2,500 (25,000 × (10% – 0%)). The benefit will cease upon repayment of the loan. Should the loan be used for a qualifying purpose then the deemed interest may qualify for a deduction. For example, if the loan is used for the purchase of a main residence, then a tax credit of £375 (2,500 × 15%) would probably be available. A loan written off after two years will be treated as additional emoluments of £25,000 at the time of write off. There will be no class 1 NIC liability as per above.

Share option scheme

The options cannot be exercised more than seven years after their grant. There will therefore be no Schedule E charge at the time that they are granted. When the options are exercised in five years time, there will be an assessment based on the market value of the shares at that date, less the amount paid for them. The assessment will therefore be £3·00 (4·00 – 1·00) for each share option exercised. There are no NIC implications. A CGT liability will arise when the shares are subsequently sold, with the shares having a base cost of £4·00 each.

(b) **(i)** *Profit related pay scheme*

(i)   At least 80% of eligible employees must be included in the scheme, although employees with less than three years service may be excluded. The proposed scheme will therefore not qualify unless it is extended to other employees.

(ii)   Employees with a material interest (25% or more of the ordinary share capital) must be excluded. This will apply to Martin Thatch.

(iii)   The PRP must be calculated by reference to the profits made by an 'employment unit'.

(iv)   A 'profit pool' must be calculated for each employment unit, and the whole of this pool paid out as PRP. The pool can be calculated as a percentage of profit made by the employment unit for the period, or as an initial sum for the first year which then varies in line with annual change in profit made by the employment unit.

(v)   The profit to be used must show a true and fair view and be calculated consistently from one year to another. The figures must be audited by an independent accountant.

(vi)   All participating employees must do so on equal terms, although variations are allowed according to length of service and level of remuneration.

Profit sharing scheme

(i)   The shares must generally be ordinary, fully paid up, and must be quoted on a recognised Stock Exchange or be shares in a company not controlled by another.

(ii)   The scheme must be run via a trust fund set up by Techno plc, which will be administered by trustees who will use funds provided by Techno plc to purchase the shares.

(iii)   The shares appropriated to employees must be retained by the trustees for at least two years.

(iv)   All employees must be given the right to participate in the scheme, although employees with less than five years service may be excluded. The proposed scheme will therefore not qualify unless it is extended to other employees.

(v)   Employees with a material interest (25% or more of the ordinary share capital) must be excluded. This will apply to Martin Thatch.

(vi)   All participating employees must do so on equal terms, although variations are allowed according to length of service and level of remuneration.

(ii) *Profit related pay scheme*

A certain amount of remuneration will be exempt from income tax. The exempt amount is the lower of £4,000 or 20% of total pay. The directors and key personnel will therefore be entitled to a tax-free amount of £4,000 each year of assessment. This is a tax saving of £1,600 p.a. (4,000 at 40%). PRP is subject to employees class 1 NIC, but there will be no additional liability as per (a).

Profit sharing scheme

The maximum market value of shares that can be allocated to a director or a key person each year of assessment is the greater of £3,000 or 10% of remuneration, subject to an overall maximum of £8,000. Provided that the shares are held by the trust for at least five years, there will be no liability to income tax.

Directors will therefore be entitled to shares worth £8,000 each year (100,000 × 10% = £10,000), which is a tax saving of £3,200 p.a. (8,000 at 40%). Key personnel will be entitled to shares worth £4,000 (40,000 × 10%) each year, which is a tax saving of £1,600 p.a. (4,000 at 40%). There will, however, be a liability to CGT. If the shares are sold after five years, the directors would have a capital gain of £24,000 (8,000 × (4 − 1)), and the key personnel a capital gain of £12,000 (4,000 × (4 − 1)).

4 **(a)** The mainstream corporation tax liability for each of companies in the Hydra Ltd group for the year ended 31 March 1996 is a follows:

	Hydra Ltd £	Boa Ltd £	Cobra Ltd £	Mamba Ltd £
Schedule D1 profit		120,000	85,000	
Capital gain	70,000			8,000
	70,000	120,000	85,000	8,000
Trade charge	(20,000)			
	50,000	120,000	85,000	8,000
Group relief				
Hydra Ltd		(45,000)		
Mamba Ltd			(12,000)	
PCTCT	50,000	75,000	73,000	8,000
CT at 25%	12,500	18,750	18,250	2,000
ACT – current year			(3,400)	
– b/f	(10,000)		(11,200)	
– surrendered				
Hydra Ltd		(13,750)		
Cobra Ltd				(1,600)
MCT	2,500	5,000	3,650	400
Trading loss c/f	15,000			
Surplus ACT c/f	8,000		800	
Capital loss c/f		15,000		

ACT workings

	Hydra Ltd £	Boa Ltd £	Cobra Ltd £	Mamba Ltd £
ACT paid				
55,000 × 20/80	13,750			
100,000 × 20/80 × 20%			5,000	
ACT brought forward	18,000		12,000	
Maximum ACT off-set				
50,000 × 20%	10,000			
75,000 × 20%		15,000		
73,000 × 20%			14,600	
8,000 × 20%				1,600

There are four associated companies in the group, so the lower limit for corporation tax purposes is £75,000 (300,000/4). Mamba Ltd is a 75% subsidiary of Cobra Ltd, but is not a 75% subsidiary of Hydra Ltd (80% × 80% = 64%). Its trading loss can therefore only be surrendered to Cobra Ltd. Hydra Ltd's trading loss of £45,000 has been surrendered to Boa Ltd in order to bring its profits down to the lower limit.

Roll-over relief has been claimed in respect of Hydra Ltd's capital gain, based on the replacement asset purchased by Boa Ltd. Since the proceeds from the disposal of Hydra Ltd's factory were £350,000, and the new office building purchased by Boa Ltd only cost £280,000, £70,000 of Hydra Ltd's capital gain cannot be rolled over.

Hydra Ltd's maximum ACT off-set is £10,000, which is less than its surplus ACT brought forward (£18,000). The maximum possible surrender (£13,750) has therefore been made to Boa Ltd. It is only possible to surrender current year ACT. Similarly, Cobra Ltd's maximum ACT off-set is £14,600, which is less than its ACT paid (£5,000) and surplus ACT brought forward (£12,000). The maximum possible surrender (£1,600) has therefore been made to Mamba Ltd. Although Cobra Ltd is included in the group income election, the proportion of its dividends paid to minority shareholders is not covered by the election. It has been assumed that neither Hydra Ltd nor Cobra Ltd can carry back ACT, since both companies have surplus ACT brought forward.

(b) (i) Mamba Ltd is a 51% subsidiary of Hydra Ltd, and therefore qualifies for the surrender of ACT and can be included in a group income election. It is also a 75% subsidiary as regards the intra-group transfer of assets. This position would not alter if the 80% shareholding in Mamba Ltd was transferred from Cobra Ltd to Hydra Ltd.

However, Mamba Ltd is not a 75% subsidiary of Hydra Ltd as regards the surrender of trading losses. Mamba Ltd can therefore only surrender trading losses to (or claim trading losses from) Cobra Ltd. For the year ended 31 March 1996 this has not affected the group's overall corporation tax liability, but it could restrict the group's flexibility in utilising trading losses in future years. Unless there are non-tax reasons for not doing so, it would be beneficial for the group to transfer the 80% shareholding in Mamba Ltd from Cobra Ltd to Hydra Ltd. This would be an intra-group transfer of assets, and so would not result in a chargeable gain or an allowable loss. It might be necessary to compensate the minority shareholders of Cobra Ltd.

(ii) The inclusion of Mamba Ltd in the group VAT registration will result in the group being partially exempt for VAT purposes. The group's recovery of input VAT would then be calculated as follows:

(1) That input tax which relates to supplies that are wholly used in making taxable supplies will be fully recoverable.

(2) That input tax which relates to supplies that are wholly used in making exempt supplies will not be recoverable.

(3) The deductible proportion of the remaining input tax is normally found using the ratio of taxable supplies to total supplies.

The inclusion of Mamba Ltd in the group VAT registration would also mean that supplies of goods and services between Mamba Ltd and the other group companies would be disregarded for VAT purposes. This will be beneficial where supplies are made to Mamba Ltd, as at present the input tax on these is not recoverable.

In order to decide if Mamba Ltd's inclusion in the group VAT registration will be beneficial, it will be necessary for the group to compare the present recovery of input tax to the prospective recovery of input tax under the above rules. It would definitely be beneficial to include Mamba Ltd in the group VAT registration if the total exempt input tax calculated under the above rules amounted to less than the *de minimis* limit of £625 per month on average, and was no more than 50% of the total input VAT. In this case, 100% of the group's input VAT would be recoverable.

5 **(a) (i)** The main reason why the Inland Revenue will have investigated Harry's accounts for the period ended 5 April 1996 is because of the fall in the GP% compared to the accounts of the previous owner. Harry's GP% is 30% (75,000/(200,000 + 50,000) × 100), compared to 41·7% (150,000/(300,000 + 60,000) × 100) for the previous owner. An analysis of the two sets of accounts shows that Harry's credit sales, cost of sales and expenses are all in line with those of the previous owner. However, Harry's cash sales are £200,000 compared to an expected £250,000 (300,000 × 10/12), which is a shortfall of £50,000. The Inland Revenue will therefore contend that cash sales of £50,000 have not been recorded. The adjustment will increase Harry's GP% to 41·7% (75,000 + 50,000/(200,000 + 50,000 + 50,000) × 100).

(ii) Harry could put forward the following criteria to justify the fall in GP% from 41·7% to 30%:

(1) He may have been selling goods at a lower margin than the previous owner.

(2) He may have been selling a different mix of goods to the previous owner (assuming that different goods have different margins).

(3) There may have been an increase in the cost price of goods which could not be passed on (or not fully passed on) to customers.

(4) He may have suffered increased theft or wastage of goods.

It will be necessary to provide evidence for any of the above criteria put forward (for example details of cost prices and selling prices), although this would be very difficult in the case of proving theft.

(b) (i) Harry will be liable to interest on overdue tax under s.86 TMA 1970. Interest will run from the original due date of 31 July 1996, as this is later than the earlier of:

(1) The actual due date. This is 30 August 1996 for the tax not postponed, and 30 January 1997 for the tax postponed.

(2) The table date of 1 July 1996.

Tax not postponed

The tax not postponed is as follows:	£
Schedule D case 1	90,000
Personal allowance	3,525
	86,475
Income tax 3,200 at 20%	640
Income tax 21,100 at 25%	5,275
Income tax 62,175 at 40%	24,870
	30,785
Less tax postponed	20,000
Tax not postponed	10,785

Interest will run from 31 July 1996 to 22 October 1996 (the date of payment), as follows:

$$£10,785 \times 10\% \times 83/365 = £245·25$$

Tax postponed

Interest will run from 31 July 1996 to 10 January 1997 (the date of payment), as follows:

£20,000 × 10% × 163/365 = £893·15

The total interest on overdue tax in respect of the 1995–96 income tax liability is £1,138·40.

(ii) Harry is liable under s.95 TMA 1970 for negligently or fraudulently submitting an incorrect return. The maximum penalty is the amount of income tax underpaid by reason of the incorrectness. This is £20,000.

The Inland Revenue will mitigate this maximum penalty depending on Harry's co-operation in the investigation, whether information was disclosed voluntarily, and to what degree his actions are considered to be fraudulent.

(c) (i) 1982 Pool

	Number	Cost	31.3.82 value
		£	£
15.6.81	25,000	25,000	31,250
Rights issue 26.1.86	75,000	375,000	375,000
	100,000	400,000	406,250
Proceeds (80,000 at 3·35)		268,000	268,000
Cost (400,000 × 80,000/100,000)		320,000	
31.3.82 value (406,250 × 80,000/100,000)			325,000
Capital loss		(52,000)	(57,000)

The indexation allowance cannot increase a loss. Harry's capital loss for 1995–96 is the lower loss of £52,000. However, since Harry's shareholding in UTC Ltd is the only chargeable asset that he held at 31 March 1982, it would be beneficial for him to elect by 5 April 1998 to have all of his gains or losses arising from assets held at 31 March 1982 to be computed by reference to their 31 March 1982 value. This would increase Harry's capital loss to £57,000.

(ii) Harry's capital loss of £57,000 can be utilised as follows:

(1) It can be set against chargeable gains, if any, for 1995–96.

(2) It can be carried forward for relief against chargeable gains (in excess of the annual exemption) of future years.

(3) As the loss is in respect of shares in an unquoted trading company, a claim can be made under s.574 ICTA 1988 by 5 April 1998 to have the capital loss set against Harry's total income of 1995–96 and/or income of 1994–95.

Unless Harry has substantial chargeable gains in 1995–96 or is anticipating them in 1996–97, it would be beneficial for Harry to claim under s.574 ICTA 1988.

If Harry wins the appeal

If the appeal is won, then Harry's total income for 1995–96 will be £40,000, compared to total income of £45,000 for 1994–95. The income tax refund will be the same whether a claim is made first against total income of 1995–96 and then against 1994–95 or vice versa. The following factors will have to be taken into account when deciding as to the order of the claims:

(1) An initial claim against total income of 1995–96 will eliminate Harry's class 4 NIC liability for that year.

(2) An initial claim against total income of 1994–95 will result in a higher repayment supplement for that year. This will run from 6 April 1996 to the end of the tax month in which repayment is made.

(3) An initial claim against total income of 1994–95 will preserve the maximum amount of total income for 1995–96 should a subsequent loss claim be made.

If Harry loses the appeal

If the appeal is lost, then Harry's total income for 1995–96 will be £90,000. The claim should therefore be made against total income of 1995–96. This would obtain tax relief at 40% for the capital loss, reducing Harry's 1995–96 income tax liability by £22,800 (57,000 at 40%). As this would eliminate the additional income tax liability for 1995–96 of £20,000, it would also eliminate the related interest charges (and possible penalties).

	£
6 (a) Deemed proceeds	320,000
Cost (60,000 × 72,000/(72,000 + 24,000))	45,000
	275,000
Indexation $45,000 \times \dfrac{148 \cdot 0 - 84 \cdot 3}{84 \cdot 3}$	34,020
	240,980
Fully chargeable 240,980 × (63 − 36)/153	42,526
Partially chargeable 240,980 × 69/153 × 20%	21,735
	64,261
CGT liability 64,261 at 40%	25,704

(b) Muriel will be entitled to roll-over relief if the 'proceeds' from the disposal of the house are 're-invested' in the ordinary share capital of an unquoted trading company. For this purpose, companies quoted on the Unlisted Securities Market do not qualify, but those quoted on the Alternative Investment Market do.

Muriel will only need to invest £64,261 in order for the entire gain to be rolled over. The gain would normally be deferred until the shares are disposed of, although further re-investment could be made at that time. There are three ways of obtaining roll-over relief:

(1) Re-investment relief

The investment must be made in the period beginning on 1 January 1995 and ending on 31 December 1998. The investment does not have to be in newly issued shares.

(2) Enterprise investment scheme (EIS)

The investment must be made in the period beginning on 1 January 1995 and ending on 31 December 1998, and the investment must be in newly issued shares. In addition to roll-over relief, Muriel will be entitled to tax relief of £12,852 (64,261 at 20%) in respect of an investment under the EIS. Provided the shares are held for five years, their disposal will be exempt from CGT. If a loss is made on the disposal of shares, then relief will be available against either capital gains or income. The calculation of the loss is based on the cost of the shares less any EIS relief obtained and not withdrawn.

(3) Venture capital trusts (VCTs)

The investment must be made in the period beginning on 1 January 1995 and ending on 31 December 1996. A VCT must have at least 70% of its investments in unquoted trading companies, and 30% of this investment must be in the form of new ordinary shares. The companies invested in must have gross assets of not more than £10 million, with the maximum investment in any one company in each tax year being £1 million. The reliefs available are similar to those under the EIS, with the addition that dividend income from a VCT is exempt from income tax. There is no requirement for the shares in a VCT to be held for five years in order for their disposal to be exempt from CGT. However, there is no relief if a loss is made on the disposal of shares in a VCT.

Conclusion

Unless Muriel wants to invest in particular unquoted companies, investment in a VCT would appear to be the most beneficial option. This is also the least riskiest method of investing in unquoted companies.

(c) In either case, Bertie will be assessed on the profits of a business of letting property under Schedule A. The assessment will be on a strict actual basis from 6 April to 5 April, and will be calculated in accordance with most of the rules used in calculating trading profits assessable under Schedule D case I. Rents will be calculated on an accruals basis.

Repairs to roof

The roof was damaged before Muriel transferred the house to Bertie. Since the roof must be repaired before the house can be let, the house would not appear to be usable at the time of the transfer. The cost of repair of £24,000 is therefore likely to be classed as capital expenditure following *Law Shipping Co Ltd v CIR* (1923). This will increase Bertie's base cost for CGT purposes.

Let as unfurnished accommodation

The cost of decoration would normally be a revenue expense. However, the house has been unoccupied since 1 October 1990, and some of the expenditure may be classed as capital if the house was in a bad state of repair on 31 December 1995. The decoration will presumably be carried out before letting commences, and so will be pre-trading expenditure. This will be allowed as an expense on the first day of business. Any capital gain arising on the disposal of the house when Bertie retires at 60, will be fully chargeable.

Let as furnished holiday accommodation

The cost of converting the house into two separate units will be mainly capital expenditure, and this will increase Bertie's base cost for CGT purposes. The figure of £41,000 may include some revenue expenditure, such as decorating costs, and this will be treated as above. The £9,000 cost of furnishing the two units will be capital expenditure. Bertie will be able to claim the following deductions from his annual gross rents of £45,000:

(i)   The loan interest of £6,000 (50,000 at 12%)

(ii) A wear and tear deduction in respect of the furniture. This will be based on either 10% of the net rent (which is likely to be 45,000 × 10% = £4,500) or on a renewals basis.

(iii) The letting agency fees of £10,125 (45,000 at 22·5%).

(iv) The other running costs of £3,500.

Expenses will be restricted if Bertie occupies the house for his own use. Given Bertie's level of rental income the letting is likely to qualify for the special rules applicable to furnished holiday lettings. This will mean that:

(i)   Capital allowance will be available on plant and machinery, such as furniture and kitchen equipment. This will almost certainly be more beneficial than the wear and tear allowance.

(ii) The Schedule A profit will qualify as net relevant earnings for personal pension purposes.

(iii) Loss relief will be available against total income.

Qualification as furnished holiday accommodation will also mean that Bertie will be entitled to retirement relief when the house is disposed of, as he will be over 55 years old at the time of disposal. He will have run the business for seven years, and so a capital gain of up to £175,000 (250,000 × 70%) will be completely exempt, with 50% of any gain in excess of this being exempt up to £525,000 (750,000 × 70%).

The letting of holiday accommodation is standard rated for VAT purposes. The forecast rental income of £45,000 is below the VAT registration limit of £46,000, but the impact of VAT will have to be considered if Bertie is already registered for VAT, or if there is an increase in rental income.

Conclusion

Letting the house as a furnished holiday letting will produce annual income of approximately £25,375 (45,000 – 6,000 – 10,125 – 3,500), compared to £28,000 if the house is let unfurnished. It will also be necessary to incur additional expenditure of £46,500 (41,000 + 9,000 – 3,500). This must be compared against the potential CGT saving upon the disposal of the house.

This marking scheme is given as a guide to markers in the context of the suggested answer. Scope is given to markers to award marks for alternative approaches to a question, including relevant comment, and where well reasoned conclusions are provided. This is particularly the case for essay based questions where there will often be more than one definitive solution.

Question 1   *Marks*

(a) *Continuation election made*

Details of continuation election	1
1996–97	1
1999–2000	1
Other years	1

Continuation election not made

Old partnership 1993–94 to 1995–96	2
Section 63 election	1
New partnership 1995–96 to 1998–99	2
1999–2000	1
Maximum/Available	10

(b) *Assessable profits*

Profits that will be assessed	1
Calculation	1
Conclusion	1

Tax liability of partners

Income tax	1
NIC	1
Total liability	1

Tax liability of Smash Ltd

Corporation tax	2
NIC	1

Tax liability of directors

Income tax /NIC	1
Total liability	1
Overall conclusion	1
Available	12
Maximum	11

		Marks
(c)	CGT implications	2
	IHT implications	2
	Maximum/Available	4
	Available	26
	Maximum	25

Question 2

(a) *Lifetime transfers*

	Marks
Gift with reservation	1
Chargeable transfer 3.12.88	1
PET 18.10.91	1
Chargeable transfer 20.4.92	2
Additional IHT	2
Due date/instalment option	1

Estate at death

	Marks
Cumulative total	1
Ordinary shares	1
Other assets/debts and funeral expenses	2
Settled property	1
Gift with reservation	1
IHT liability	1
Rate of IHT on estate	1
IHT due by estate/due date	1
Harold's inheritance	1
Other IHT liabilities/due dates	2
Available	20
Maximum	17

		Marks
(b)	Income tax treatment	2
	Variation of terms of will	2
	Maximum/Available	4

			Marks
(c)	Banks/building societies/National Savings		2
	Unit trusts/investment trusts/equity shares/PEPs		3
		Available	5
		Maximum	4
		Available	29
		Maximum	25

Question 3

(a)	Profit related pay scheme		2
	Profit sharing scheme		2
	Company motor cars		4
	Beneficial loans		3
	Share option scheme		3
		Available	14
		Maximum	13

(b)	**(i)**	*Profit related pay scheme*	
		Eligible/participating employees	2
		Employment units	1
		Profit pool/calculation of profit	1
		Profit sharing scheme	
		Shares/trust fund	1
		Retention of shares	1
		Right to participate	1
		Employees with a material interest	1
		Participating employees	1

		Available	9
		Maximum	7

		Marks
(ii)	Profit related pay scheme	2
	Profit sharing scheme – income tax	3
	– CGT	1
	Available	6
	Maximum	5
	Available	29
	Maximum	25

Question 4

(a)	Schedule DI profit	1
	Capital gains/roll-over relief	2
	Trade charge	1
	Group relief	4
	Corporation tax	1
	ACT – Hydra Ltd	4
	– Boa Ltd/Mamba Ltd	1
	– Cobra Ltd	4
	Amounts carried forward	2
	Available	20
	Maximum	18

(b)	*Transfer of shareholding*	
	Present position	1
	Surrender of trading losses	1
	Conclusion	1
	Intra-group transfer	1
	Group VAT registration	
	VAT recovery if partially exempt	2
	Intra-group supplies	1
	Conclusion	1
	De minimis limit	2
	Available	10
	Maximum	7
	Available	30
	Maximum	25

Question 5

(a) *Reason for investigation*

Discussion of GP%	2
Shortfall in cash sales	2
Impact of adjustment	1

Justification of profits

Lower margin/different mix	1
Increase in cost price/theft	1
Evidence	1
Available	8
Maximum	5

(b) *Interest on overdue tax*

Due date	2
Interest on tax not postponed	3
Interest on tax postponed	2

Penalty

Maximum penalty	1
Mitigation	1
Maximum/Available	9

(c) *Capital loss*

1982 pool	2
Calculation of capital loss	2
31 March 1982 election	1

Utilisation of loss

Chargeable gains/carry forward	1
Claim under s.574 ICTA 1988	2

If the appeal is won

Income tax refund	1
Factors to consider	2

If the appeal is lost		*Marks*
Claim against total income of 1995–96		1
Tax relief		1
Impact on interest and penalty		1
		___
	Available	14
		___
	Maximum	11
		___
	Available	31
		___
	Maximum	25
		___

Question 6

(a) Calculation of capital gain — 2

CGT liability — 2

Maximum/Available — 4

(b) Qualifying investments — 1

Amount to be invested/deferral — 1

Re-investment relief

Period of investment/qualifying shares — 1

Enterprise investment scheme

Period of investment/qualifying shares — 1

Other reliefs available — 2

Venture capital trusts

Period of investment — 1

Description of VCT — 2

Other reliefs available — 1

Available — 10

Maximum — 8

		Marks
(c) Basis of assessment		1
Repairs to roof		
Classification as capital expenditure		1
Let as unfurnished accommodation		
Decoration costs		2
Capital gain		1
Let as furnished holiday accommodation		
Coversion costs		1
Furnishings		1
Deductions		2
Furnished holiday letting – reliefs		2
Capital gain/retirement relief		2
VAT		1
Conclusion		1
	Available	15
	Maximum	13
	Available	29
	Maximum	25